Pharmaceutical Price Regulation

Pharmaceutical Price Regulation

National Policies versus Global Interests

Patricia M. Danzon

The AEI Press

Publisher for the American Enterprise Institute
WASHINGTON, D.C.

1997

To order call toll free 1-800-462-6420 or 1-717-794-3800. For all other inquiries please contact the AEI Press, 1150 Seventeenth Street, N.W., Washington, D.C. 20036 or call 1-800-862-5801.

Library of Congress Cataloging-in-Publication Data

Danzon, Patricia Munch, 1946—
    Pharmaceutical price regulation: national policies versus global interests / Patricia M. Danzon.
        p.   cm.
    Includes bibliographical references (p.   ).
    ISBN 0-8447-3982-0 (alk. paper).—ISBN 0-8447-3983-9 (pbk. : alk. paper)
        1. Drugs—Prices—United States.   2. Pharmaceutical industry—United States.   3. Pharmaceutical policy—United States.
    HD9666.4.D36   1996
    338.4'36151'0973—DC20   96-12144
                                                                        CIP

THE AEI PRESS
Publisher for the American Enterprise Institute
1150 17th Street, N.W., Washington, D.C. 20036

Contents

FIGURES

1
Introduction

The regulation of drug prices and expenditures is becoming increasingly stringent in many countries, as governments attempt new strategies to control their health care spending. These foreign systems have attracted attention as possible models for the regulation of drug prices in the United States. Recent studies have argued that prices in other countries are lower because of price regulation (for example, GAO [1992, 1994a, b]). President Clinton's Health Security Act called for the creation of an Advisory Council on Breakthrough Drugs that would evaluate the reasonableness of new drug prices, based on costs and the lowest price charged in more than twenty other countries, extending a similar model used in Canada. Although the threat of drug price controls has receded in the United States, it will doubtless return if (or when) attention reverts to the issue of adding outpatient drug coverage to Medicare or expanding health insurance more generally. Meanwhile, market-driven controls through managed drug benefit programs are spreading rapidly and becoming more stringent in private insurance plans.

These trends raise important questions about the effects of different schemes for controlling drug spending. How successful have various regulatory strategies been in controlling drug expenditures? How are the various forms of regulation, on the one hand, and managed-care strategies, on the other hand, likely to affect the incentives and ability of the research-based pharmaceutical industry to sustain innovative R&D? In what other ways do these con-

1

trols affect efficiency in the pharmaceutical industry and in the delivery of health care?

These foreign regulatory schemes are of interest to the United States not only because they are possible models for health care cost control but also because these schemes already affect U.S. drug manufacturers and ultimately U.S. consumers. U.S. firms are the major producers of innovative drugs, and innovative drugs are truly global products. U.S. firms have been responsible for the discovery of more than 40 percent of innovative drugs in the last three decades (Barral 1995; CBO 1994; Redwood 1993). Innovator firms market these drugs worldwide, either through outlicensing to foreign firms or through their own foreign subsidiaries.[1] Thus, price controls in any major market of the world affect the returns to innovator firms, regardless of their country of origin, and U.S. firms are the leading players in this field.

This direct effect of one country's regulation on firms based in another country is expanding with multiplier effects due to the indirect spillovers from the regulatory use of international price comparisons and from parallel trade. Canada and Italy, for example, already use foreign prices to set regulatory limits on their domestic drug prices. Similar schemes have been proposed for Japan, the second largest market in the world. In the United States, the international price comparisons proposed in President Clinton's Health Security Act could have limited U.S. prices to the levels that prevail in traditionally low-priced countries such as Spain. At the same time, the threat from parallel trade—whereby importers purchase drugs in countries with low prices, usually due to regulation, and resell them in countries with higher prices—is increasing with the accession to the European Union (EU) of tradi-

---

1. Pirating without license in countries that do not enforce intellectual property rights is also a major source of drug diffusion but one that generates no revenues to originator firms.

tionally low-price countries such as Spain and, in the future, countries of Eastern Europe. Although so far pharmaceuticals are not included in the North American Free Trade Agreement (NAFTA), the pressure to permit parallel trade within and between other trading blocs is likely to grow.

The high cost of R&D makes pharmaceuticals particularly vulnerable to aggressive price regulation and that makes the cross-national equalization of prices potentially harmful rather than beneficial to consumers. For U.S. drug companies, the ratio of R&D to current sales is roughly 18 percent (CBO 1994), higher than for any other industry. Converting all costs for a cohort of drugs to present value at the date of launch, R&D is roughly 30 percent of total costs. These R&D costs are global joint costs that are essential to supply the drug but cannot rationally be attributed to any individual consumer or country. Moreover, these costs are sunk at the point of price negotiation. At the limit, companies would rationally continue to make existing drugs available as long as prices cover country-specific marginal cost, but this marginal cost could be as low as 25 percent of total costs.

The low ratio of marginal cost to sunk, joint costs gives any powerful drug purchaser an incentive to try to drive prices down to the marginal cost of serving their patient population, leaving others to pay the joint costs of R&D. Small countries such as New Zealand can pursue this strategy with a negligible effect on global incentives for drug innovation as long as markets remain separate. The effects of these strategies expand, however, and affect consumers worldwide once spillovers become common and markets are no longer separable because of parallel trade and regulation based on international price comparisons.

This study examines the effects of different forms of drug price regulation, first in the context of a single closed economy and then in the more realistic context of

3

a global economy with connected markets. Using economic theory and empirical evidence, we examine the effects of various forms of regulation on incentives for innovation and on production efficiency. Certain forms of regulation are found to be particularly biased against innovative R&D, favoring imitative R&D that attempts only minor modifications of known substances. Certain regulations also tend to favor domestic firms at the expense of international firms, contrary to international requirements for transparency and regulatory neutrality.

The empirical evidence shows that even stringent price regulatory systems have failed in their primary goal of controlling total drug expenditures. Countries are therefore moving to more comprehensive strategies, such as global drug budgets, that control volumes or total expenditures directly. The preliminary evidence indicates that these new regulatory strategies are more effective at controlling public drug spending, but are likely to have adverse effects on the quality of patient care and on incentives for innovative R&D.

The challenge for public policy is to find an appropriate balance between controlling health care spending today and preserving incentives for innovative R&D that can improve health and the quality of life in the future. Most regulatory strategies, however, tend to be biased toward short-run cost control. These regulatory strategies resemble in certain ways some of the control mechanisms used by private pharmacy benefit managers in the United States. Theory suggests, however, that the competitive approach, applied at the level of the individual health plan, is more likely to preserve incentives for the efficient use of drugs and appropriate incentives for innovation than is the regulatory approach, applied at the level of government. Empirical testing of these hypotheses remains an important subject for future research.

2
The Economics of Pharmaceutical Costs and Pricing

The pharmaceutical industry is more research intensive than any other industry, with roughly 18 percent of current pharmaceutical sales spent on R&D (CBO 1994). If all costs including R&D, marketing, and production for a cohort of drugs are expressed in discounted present value at the time of launch, however, then R&D accounts for roughly 30 percent of total costs, manufacturing and distribution are 29 percent, marketing is 24 percent, and other administrative costs are 12 percent (table 2–1).[1]

The Cost Structure of Innovative Pharmaceuticals

The R&D cost per new chemical entity (NCE) brought to market in the United States was estimated in 1993 at $359 million before taxes, $194 million after taxes (OTA 1993). One major factor contributing to these high R&D costs is the number of "dry holes"—compounds investigated but subsequently abandoned in the search for products that are safe, effective, and truly innovative. A second major factor is the capital cost (forgone interest) of funds tied

---

1. These estimates are based on cost data from U.S. Office of Technology Assessment (1993), as reported in Danzon (1994). The data are after taxes, assuming a 46 percent corporate tax rate, and a 10 percent cost of capital. The pretax figure for R&D is 32 percent. I would like to thank Dan Zhang for assistance in developing these estimates.

TABLE 2-1
THE COST STRUCTURE OF PHARMACEUTICALS: DISCOUNTED
PRESENT VALUE AT LAUNCH
(percentage of total cost after tax)

	Tax Assumptions	
Cost Component	46% corporate tax	46% corporate tax, plus R&D and possessions tax credits
Total R&D cost	31.1	29.7
R&D	29.0	27.6
Ongoing R&D costs	2.1	2.1
Total manufacturing cost	28.2	28.7
Manufacturing and distribution	25.3	25.8
Capital expenditure (plant and equipment)	2.9	2.9
Other		
Marketing costs	23.4	23.9
General and administrative costs	11.5	11.7
Working capital	3.3	3.4
Value of inventory	2.4	2.6
Total	100	100

NOTE: Assumes 10 percent cost of capital.
SOURCE: Data from OTA (1993).

up because of the lag—averaging twelve years in the
United States—between the initiation of R&D and the
launch of a successful product. These costs of R&D appear
to be rising over time. Although techniques of rational
drug design should reduce the costs of discovering and
evaluating promising leads, this advantage appears to be
more than offset by rising input costs and increasing regulatory requirements, including larger and longer clinical
trials that are needed to ensure safety and efficacy of

drugs for chronic conditions.[2]

Both cost factors are expected to be higher, on average, for truly innovative drugs than for minor modifications of existing compounds. False leads—and hence the risk and average cost per successful new drug—are likely to be more frequent for research that targets new compounds or new modes of action rather than minor extensions. This, in turn, raises the time and capital costs of development.[3] Consistent with this, DiMasi and others (1991) report higher input costs for drugs ranked by the Food and Drug Administration as significant innovations than for drugs ranked as not innovative.

The large R&D share of total costs raises problems for pricing because R&D is a global joint cost, that is, the cost is the same regardless of the number of users served worldwide and hence cannot rationally be allocated to particular users. Production and distribution also entail significant costs that jointly serve several countries. Primary production of bulk chemicals is typically concentrated in two or three plants worldwide, each of which

2. The actual average cost per NCE, of course, results from corporate decisions as to which compounds are worthwhile to pursue. If regulation or competition leads to a decline in expected revenues per approved drug, then average costs of R&D ex post will likely decline. This shift, however, would reflect the elimination of compounds that were perceived as too risky or too costly to develop, given the lower expected returns. Thus, one can interpret the $359 million figure as the cost of R&D to produce the rate of innovation that was achieved in the 1970s and 1980s.

3. This capital cost accounts for roughly half of total cost (DiMasi et al. 1991). The costs of delay may be reduced by pursuing more stages of the R&D simultaneously rather than sequentially, but a simultaneous strategy increases risk and does not necessarily reduce total costs. If regulatory authorities grant priority to innovative products, the tendency for more innovative products to entail higher time costs may be mitigated, but the higher risks are not. Moreover, innovative products may face greater delay in getting price approval in regulatory regimes, offsetting any gain from priority in registration.

serves all countries in an entire region and produces multiple compounds for many years. The capital costs of such plants cannot be attributed to specific packs of particular drugs sold in, say, France or Italy in 1995. Distribution networks and other overhead may be country specific but often cannot be attributed precisely to specific products sold in that country.

The problem of pricing in the presence of joint costs is exacerbated by the fact that most of the joint costs, including expenditures on R&D, production capacity, promotion, and other overhead, are largely committed (sunk) before the initial price negotiations take place. The ratio of sunk costs to marginal (incremental) costs increases over the life of a drug. This high percentage of sunk, joint costs creates a great temptation for exploitation by regulators. For any firm, the profit-maximizing strategy is to supply a product as long as the price covers the marginal cost per unit, even if that price is less than average total cost including the sunk costs. Any amount greater than the marginal cost contributes to paying off the sunk costs. In the long run, however, if the firm is to stay in business and continue to develop new products, the average price across all units in all markets must be sufficient to cover the average total cost, including the joint costs.

Patents as a Means of Recouping R&D Costs. R&D costs are, of course, not unique to drugs, although they are a higher percentage of total costs. In most industrialized countries, patent protection provides a legal means whereby innovators may earn a reasonable return on their R&D investments. If imitators could immediately copy a new invention, competition would force prices down to marginal production cost, and the innovator could not recover the cost of R&D. With patent protection, however, the innovator may be able to price above marginal cost for the duration of the patent, depending on the extent of competition from close substitutes. Whether the actual duration of the patent is adequate, excessive, or insufficient to encourage an optimal rate of innovation is theoretically indeterminate and varies across industries and products, depending on competition from closely substitutable products.

In the case of drugs, however, the value of patent protection is further limited by regulatory constraints. Severe price regulation in some countries is now spilling over to other, less regulated markets, through parallel imports and international price comparisons.

The Economics and Politics of Drug Price Regulation

Drug price regulation constrains through one branch of government the value of the patents that are granted through another branch of government. Regulation of pharmaceutical prices cannot be justified on grounds of natural monopoly, which is the traditional rationale for the regulation of power generation and telecommunications. Any monopoly power enjoyed by pharmaceuticals derives from the patent protection that is granted by the state to encourage innovation.

The primary rationale for the regulation of drug prices derives from government's role in funding social insurance schemes that cover outpatient drugs. Insurance coverage for drugs, like other medical services, tends to make consumers indifferent to costs because "someone else is paying." Similarly, medical providers have financial incentives to prescribe drugs without regard to cost if patients are thereby encouraged to make more visits and visits are reimbursed on a fee-for-service basis. This "moral hazard effect"—that insurance tends to encourage overuse of covered services by consumers and providers— leads public and private insurers to attempt to limit the services that they reimburse and the prices that they pay, particularly in countries where copayments are minimal, after exemptions and supplementary insurance are taken into account.

Economic theory concludes that some well-designed strategies to constrain moral hazard are desirable when insurers cannot perfectly monitor inappropriate use of insured services. Constraints on moral hazard are in the long-run interests of consumers, who ultimately pay for overuse through higher premiums or higher taxes.[4] These strategies ideally target consumer incentives through co-payments and provider incentives through capitation, information-based utilization controls, and so forth. The optimal mix of controls balances the gains from controlling overuse against the disutility to patients from exposure to out-of-pocket costs and restrictions on their choice of services.

Optimal controls on moral hazard in a dynamic environment must also balance the control of current budgetary costs against the need to preserve efficient incentives for R&D since R&D is critical to the quality of services available in the future. In social insurance systems, however, the government, as the monopsony purchaser for pharmaceuticals, has strong incentives to focus on its country-specific short-run interests of controlling its own pharmaceutical budget, assuming that its contributions have negligible effect on manufacturers' incentives for R&D that derive from their global revenues. Thus, each country attempts to drive prices down to the marginal cost of supplying that country, ignoring global joint costs.

How inadequate could prices be if all users paid only their marginal cost? The estimates in table 2–1 suggest that if all purchasers paid only their short-run, user-specific marginal cost, including the cost of secondary production and distribution, the shortfall between revenues and total costs could be as high as 70 percent. If prices

---

4. Zeckhauser (1970) describes optimal patient copayment; Ellis and McGuire (1993) consider optimal provider cost-sharing.

covered all costs except R&D, the shortfall would be roughly 30 percent. A further implication of the low ratio of user-specific marginal cost to total costs is that if prices are adequate to cover the joint sunk costs, they will appear to yield abnormally high accounting "profits."[5] The perception of high accounting profit in the pharmaceutical industry further fuels the arguments for lower prices.

Other industries that have traditionally been subject to price regulation, including telephone, gas, and electricity, are also characterized by a high proportion of sunk, capital costs to user-specific marginal costs. For utilities, however, these capital costs are generally country specific and must clearly be paid for by the consumers served locally if they are to continue to receive services. The regulatory formulas for setting utility prices generally recognize the need to provide a reasonable return on capital. Thus, it is the *global* nature of the sunk, joint costs of pharmaceuticals that makes the regulation of drug prices potentially more distortionary than the regulation of traditional utilities.

Optimal Pricing to Share Joint Costs

Economic theory has well-established principles for efficient pricing to share joint costs, known as Ramsey pricing, after economist Frank Ramsey (Ramsey 1927). Contrary to the common presumption, these principles imply that to charge all users the same price is not optimal. Rather, users whose demand is relatively price inelastic should pay higher prices than users whose demand is relatively price elastic.

These Ramsey pricing principles are commonly applied in public utilities, airlines, and other industries with significant joint costs relative to user-specific marginal

---

5. For analysis of the bias in reported rates of return on equity that results from intangible assets, see Clarkson (1996) and CBO (1994).

costs. Peak-time users pay higher prices for electricity than do off-peak users. Travelers with inelastic demand pay higher airfares than travelers who are willing to accept the inconvenience of advanced booking and minimum stay requirements. Although those who pay more may grumble, their prices can be lower than they would have to be to cover the costs of the same level of service in the absence of the discount fares. This is true as long as the discount fares cover their own marginal costs and make some contribution to the joint costs.

Applying these principles to the problem of paying for the joint costs of pharmaceutical R&D, efficiency requires that consumers who value innovative drugs more highly and hence have less price-elastic demand should pay higher prices than consumers whose demand is more price elastic. With a uniform price, those with the highest valuation pay less than their true marginal benefit (willingness to pay). Those with lower valuation face a price that exceeds their willingness to pay and hence will reduce their use or drop out of the market entirely—even though they might have been willing to pay a price that covered the marginal costs of serving them and even though their use adds nothing to the joint costs.[6]

Total revenues are higher with differential pricing, both because those consumers with higher valuation pay more and because those with low valuation now stay in the market. The higher revenue with differential pricing can support a higher rate of investment in R&D and hence lead to a greater flow of innovative drugs. Uniform prices would make it uneconomic to develop some innovative

6. Similarly, prices may optimally differ among consumers within the same country, depending on their price sensitivity. Some consumers, for example, are willing to accept restrictions on choice in managed-care plans in return for lower-priced coverage. Thus, the existence of drug price discounts to managed care plans in the United States is consistent with Ramsey pricing principles. This does not mean that actual price differentials are necessarily optimal.

drugs that consumers in aggregate would have been willing to pay for, with positive net benefit, had differential pricing been feasible.

Unfortunately, consumers' true willingness to pay is unobservable, so application of these principles in practice is necessarily imperfect. Willingness to pay may depend on income, on preferences for comfort and convenience, on attitudes toward risk and toward medical care in general. Consumers and their third-party payers may rationally attempt to conceal their own willingness to pay, as long as others are willing to cover the common costs. But, in the long run, everyone is worse off from this free-rider strategy. Even if the unobservability of true preferences makes it impossible to match price differentials perfectly with willingness to pay, recognition by policy makers of the general principles of optimal price differentials would be a valuable first step.

A further implication of the high proportion of globally joint costs and Ramsey principles for pricing to cover such costs is that any attempt to regulate drug prices on the basis of costs—as attempted in Italy before 1993 and proposed by President Clinton—lacks an economic foundation. No accounting rule can determine the fraction of the joint costs that should be paid by Italians or Americans—rather, optimal shares should be determined from the demand structure. Any attempt to regulate drug prices on the basis of costs is fundamentally arbitrary and therefore open to political influence and abuse, as the Italian corruption scandal of 1993 has demonstrated.

Summary

The pharmaceutical industry's high ratio of globally joint, sunk costs—mostly R&D—to user-specific, marginal costs creates the temptation and leverage for regulators and major purchasers to force prices down to marginal cost.

Pure marginal cost pricing would cover roughly 30 percent or less of total cost.

Optimal pricing to cover the joint costs of R&D requires that prices differ among consumer groups, based on their price elasticity of demand. Uniform prices are not optimal, contrary to common presumption. Uniform pricing would result in lower global revenues; some innovative drugs would not be developed—drugs that consumers would have been willing to pay for, had differential pricing based on willingness to pay been feasible.

3
Regulation of Pharmaceutical Prices and Expenditures

The Objectives of Price Regulation

Regulation of drug prices and expenditures has grown out of government's role in social insurance programs. The primary objective of drug price regulation is to control public spending on drugs. Social insurance programs generally cover outpatient drugs. Like any insurer, public insurers have attempted to limit either the prices of covered services or the reimbursement paid by the public program. Over time, however, such controls have become increasingly stringent, and controls on volumes and total expenditures are being superimposed because price controls alone have failed to control total spending. These additional measures include drug budgets, both global and per physician, and total revenue caps for pharmaceutical manufacturers. Thus, the legitimate desire to control insurance-induced moral hazard on the part of patients and providers is evolving into multiple tiers of regulation that are insensitive to the needs of individual patients, with adverse effects on efficiency and innovation.

A second objective of price regulatory schemes in some countries is to promote industrial policy goals of domestic employment, investment, and international competitiveness. The price regulatory schemes in France and Italy, for example, grant higher prices for products that are produced domestically (Burstall and Reuben 1988);

the United Kingdom regulates the rate of return on capital within the country, a practice that rewards investments in the U.K. As in other industries, such input-based regulation distorts productive efficiency.

This chapter provides a brief overview of the main forms of regulation as the groundwork for understanding their effects.

Forms of Price Regulation

Direct Price Regulation. France, Italy, and Spain require that prices of new products and price changes of existing products be approved if they are to be reimbursed by the social insurance system. Inflation adjustments are rarely granted, and across-the-board price cuts are sometimes mandated. Wholesale and retail distribution margins are also regulated, such that government controls the retail prices charged to insurers or consumers.

These regulatory schemes use multiple criteria for setting prices. Before 1993, Italy used a complex pricing formula based on costs, with markups for therapeutic merit and contribution to the domestic economy. Despite the apparent detailed objectivity of such a formula, in fact any estimate of costs depends critically on the value assigned to R&D, which is theoretically indeterminate (see chapter 2) but in practice depends on the transfer pricing rules for primary ingredients. The arbitrary and subjective nature of such a scheme is evidenced by the 1993 corruption scandal concerning Italy's price review board, which sent most members to jail. Since 1993, Italy has used international price comparisons as a basis for setting domestic prices. A key question here is whether prices should be compared based on exchange rates or purchasing power parities (this is discussed further in chapter 6).

France has traditionally regulated prices using several criteria, including internal comparisons with existing products; therapeutic merit; and contribution to the domestic economy. In addition, for drugs that account for a significant fraction of expenditures, an "envelope globale" applies a comprehensive revenue limit: if volume is higher than targeted, the price is cut to bring the government's total spending on the drug within the target. In 1994, manufacturer revenue limits were superimposed on the price regulatory scheme (see below).

Canada operates a somewhat looser form of price control. The Patented Medicines Review Board monitors prices of new products to determine whether they are "reasonable." The benchmark for innovative products is the median of prices charged in nine other countries; for products that represent only minor or no therapeutic advance over existing drugs, prices are tied to the prices of these existing drugs. Postlaunch price increases may not exceed the growth of the general consumer price index. Before 1993, the penalties for "unreasonable" prices included compulsory licensing, which effectively nullifies patent protection.

In the United States, President Clinton's Health Security Act proposed an Advisory Council on Breakthrough New Drugs to evaluate the reasonableness of the prices of new drugs. This proposal included elements of several foreign systems. Reasonableness was to be evaluated based on several criteria, including cost and international comparisons, based on the *lowest* price in a group of more than twenty countries. If a price were deemed unreasonable, the drug could be denied reimbursement under public programs. The act also proposed a mandatory 17 percent rebate for the new Medicare drug benefit and an additional excess-inflation rebate on any drug whose price increased more rapidly than general inflation. These rebate proposals mirrored similar rebates that have been required for Medicaid and other public programs since 1989. Although prices charged to these public programs are not regulated directly, manufacturers are required to pay "best price" rebates, equal to the greater of their best

17

discount to a private purchaser or 15 percent, and an excess inflation rebate.

None of these regulatory criteria for setting prices are based on a coherent framework that adequately recognizes the problem of global joint costs. In practice, these prices rely ultimately on negotiation and political discretion, notwithstanding the transparency directive of the European Economic Community (EEC). Prices based on international price comparisons appear to be more objective, but in practice the methods of such comparisons leave much room for judgment because countries differ in their mixture of dosage forms and strengths (see chapter 4)—for example, is the comparison on the basis of price per gram, per unit, or per pack? using exchange rates or purchasing power parities? In any case, there is no economic rationale for preferring uniform prices. On the contrary, prices should optimally differ depending on how different countries value innovative drugs (see chapter 2). Price negotiations entail uncertainty and delay, over and above the delay associated with obtaining approval of safety, efficacy, and quality. Delay in the launch of new products results in forgone benefits for consumers and in loss of revenue for manufacturers that cannot be recouped because the patent clock continues to tick while pricing approval is awaited.

Manufacturer-Specific Budgets (Revenue Limits). In 1994, France adopted an accord between government and industry that grants manufacturers more pricing freedom in return for government control on total drug spending. The government sets a target rate of growth for general pharmaceutical expenditures (3–4 percent for 1994). It then negotiates with each manufacturer a firm-specific limit on the firm's total sales (revenue) growth for the year. If the firm overshoots its target, then its prices are reduced. This system was intended to give manufacturers greater flexibility in pricing individual products, subject to their general revenue limit, and hence reduce the uncertainty and administrative cost of product-by-product price negotiations. It remains to be seen how much flexibility will, in fact, be permitted—requirements for individual price approval apparently remain for major drugs. The 1994 accord also included agreements for restraint on promotional expenditures, improved information systems, and attempts to limit prescribing to medically appropriate uses.

Reference Price Limits on Reimbursement. Reference price reimbursement systems have been introduced in Germany, the Netherlands, Denmark, New Zealand, and British Columbia. Drugs are grouped into clusters with therapeutically similar properties. The government or insurer sets a single reimbursement price (reference price) for all products in a cluster. In theory, the manufacturer is free to charge a price above the reference price, but, in that case, the patient must pay the difference as an excess out-of-pocket charge.[1] In Germany, physicians are required by law to explain to patients why such a charge is necessary. In practice, manufacturers rarely charge more than the reference price, presumably because the time requirements for physicians and patients' reluctance to pay excess copayments make demand highly elastic at prices above the reference price (Danzon and Liu 1996).

Although reference pricing invokes competition between products within a cluster for prices above the reference price, it may actually reduce competition below the reference price. In any industry, manufacturers have an incentive to cut price if demand is elastic (that is, the price cut generates at least an equiproportionate increase in volume). But in the German reference price system, de-

---

1. Maximum allowable charge (MAC) systems used in many Medicaid and managed-care programs in the United States are similar but apply only to generic substitutes.

19

mand is inelastic at prices below the reference price because any difference between the manufacturer price and the reference price accrues to the government and hence has no effect on incentives of any of the parties who could affect volume—physicians who prescribe, pharmacists who dispense, and patients who consume the drugs. Not surprisingly, prices of generic drugs have fallen less than prices of originator drugs under the German reference price system (Maassen 1995; Danzon and Liu 1996). In the Netherlands, since pharmacists retain 20 percent (previously 30 percent) of the margin between the reference price and the wholesale price, they have an incentive to seek out and switch patients to lower-priced generics and parallel imports.

The impact of reference price systems on drug spending depends on how broadly the clusters are defined and how the reference price is set. Phase 1 of the German system and most Medicaid programs in the United States apply only to generically equivalent products, for which the patent has expired. The potential impact is much greater—for payers, consumers, and manufacturers—if reference pricing is extended to products that have different active ingredients but are deemed therapeutically similar. Phase 2 in Germany included products within a similar chemical class, such as benzodiazepines and H2 antagonists. Phase 3 extends to products that are deemed close therapeutic substitutes by regulatory agencies. Phases 2 and 3 can thus apply to compounds that may have different therapeutic benefits and side effects for at least some consumers. By July 1994, reference pricing applied to 62 percent of the market in Germany (Maassen 1995), and this is expected to grow.

The German reference price system failed to achieve the desired slowdown in drug spending in part because of upgrading in the mix of drugs and continued volume growth. In 1993, the German government implemented a 5 percent price rollback, a price freeze through 1994, increased consumer copayments for drugs, and a total limit on total 1993 drug spending, set at the 1991 spending levels. If the target is exceeded, physicians and drug manufacturers contribute to the overrun (see below).

Rate-of-Return Regulation. The U.K. Pharmaceutical Price Regulation Scheme regulates profits, not prices. Under the PPRS, companies are free to set launch prices of new products, provided that the total rate of return on capital (ROC) on their portfolio of products reimbursed by the National Health Service (NHS) does not exceed a specified limit. Each company negotiates with the government for an allowed ROC, within the range of 17–21 percent. There is a gray area within which a company may, after renegotiation, retain some or part of any profit above the target. Any excess is "repaid" either directly or through a price reduction. Conversely, companies that fail to meet their target ROC may apply for a price increase. In 1993, this gray area was reduced from 50 percent to 25 percent of the target ROC. Reimbursement prices of off-patent drugs are regulated by the Drug Tariff. Prices of nonprescription (over-the-counter or OTC) drugs are unregulated.

The goals of the PPRS are "to secure the provision of safe and effective medicines for the National Health Service at reasonable prices; . . . and to promote a strong and profitable pharmaceutical industry in the UK capable of such sustained R&D expenditures as should lead to the future availability of new and improved medicines" (1993 PPRS revisions). Although this system of profit control more explicitly recognizes the need to provide a fair return on R&D than do most systems of price control, it has other potentially distorting effects. Rate-of-return regulation is notorious for creating incentives for creative accounting to maximize reimbursement and, more seriously, for distorting incentives for real resource use to maximize the rate base and hence the allowed profit.[2]

Not surprisingly, the regulations have become increasingly detailed over time. There are rules for allocation of costs between the NHS and exports, for allowable promotional expenditures, etc. An allowable R&D expenditure limit is negotiated with each company for the next year and provisional targets for the following two years, up to a maximum of 22.5 percent of sales to the NHS. The limits for promotion and R&D do not apply to actual expenditures but to the amount that can be included in the base of the ROC calculation. These limits can be particularly binding for smaller companies introducing new products because of the high cost of application for marketing authorization[3] and postmarketing surveillance. Nevertheless, compared with direct price regulation, the PPRS entails much lower transactions costs, requiring only aggregate data from annual financial statements, not on individual drugs, and less delay and uncertainty over the timing and price of launch of new products.

The PPRS appears to have been relatively successful at controlling drug expenditures, which account for only 10 percent of NHS spending, or 0.59 percent of the U.K. gross domestic product in 1992. This control implies low real spending per capita relative to other countries, despite minimal copayment (83 percent of prescription items in 1991 were exempt from copayments, hence free to the consumer). Many factors contribute to this low per capita spending on drugs in addition to the PPRS, including conservative medical norms and slow adoption of new therapies; capitation of general practitioners (GPs), who

---

2. See, for example, Averch and Johnson (1962).

3. The most recent estimate is £96,000 (Association of the British Pharmaceutical Industry 1993). This number is not directly comparable with the much higher estimate for the United States of $359 million (before tax) per approved NCE (OTA 1993) because the U.S. figure includes the allocated cost of dry holes and the time cost of money, which may be excluded from the U.K. figure.

have less incentive to use prescriptions to encourage patient visits than do physicians who are paid fee-for-service; and incentives for physicians and pharmacists to substitute generics, for which prices are regulated. In 1992, 43 percent of all prescriptions and 35 percent of dispensed items were dispensed generically (ABPI 1993), a situation roughly comparable with the United States.[4] As in the United States, these percentages are expected to increase dramatically as many major products go off patent within the next few years.[5]

Despite the low absolute drug expenditures per capita in the U.K., the real rate of growth of spending on pharmaceuticals was about 3–5 percent a year for the period 1979–1990. This trend prompted the Department of Health (DOH) to introduce new measures, including dissemination of drug price comparison data and monitoring of individual physicians for deviations from the norms of prescribing for their specialty. So far, these are merely "indicative budgets," with no financial sanctions for overruns, except for fundholding GPs (see below). Real spending fell 1.3 percent for 1990–1991.

Nevertheless, the October 1993 revision of the PPRS provides for a 2.5 percent price reduction;[6] a three-year price freeze; a reduction of the gray area to 25 percent of ROC; elimination of the promotion allowance for new NCEs[7] and a mandatory rebate if sales of a new drug ex-

---

4. U.S. Congressional Budget Office (1994).

5. Between 1992 and 2000, 54 of the 100 most popular drugs in the United States, which account for a similar share of sales, are expected to go off patent (Congressional Budget Office 1994).

6. This reduction is to be achieved by either an across-the-board 2.5 percent reduction on all products, a set of changes that produces an average 2.5 percent reduction, or cash rebates in lieu of price decreases. The latter approach avoids cross-national spillover effects of changing prices.

7. Previously, the formula for allowable promotional expense included an NCE allowance of £1.5m. over two years. The full formula (excluding the NCE allowance) is a fixed base of £600,000 + 6 percent

ceed £12 million in any of the first five years after launch; and stricter promotional expense limits. In addition, the NHS has increased incentives for generic substitution and has expanded its blacklist, which limits reimbursement for certain categories of drugs to a few generics.

Physician Drug Budgets. The most potent weapon discovered so far in governments' battle to control drug spending is to place physicians directly at risk for the financial consequences of their prescribing habits. Even physicians who do not profit directly from dispensing drugs may use prescriptions as a means of stimulating additional patient visits, particularly if a patient visit to obtain or renew a prescription is reimbursed fee-for-service and entails minimal cost in the physician's time.[8]

Governments have, therefore, acted on physician incentives to control drug spending. In Germany, if total drug spending exceeds the target drug budget, the first 280 million deutsche marks are charged to the physician budget for the following year. The next 280 million deutsche marks are charged to drug manufacturers to reduce their incentives for drug promotion. In the first six months since the introduction of the drug budget in 1993, the rate of spending fell 18 percent below the rate for the same period the prior year. Since 1995, individual physicians are also assigned budgets based on their specialty. Deviations of more than 25 percent from the mean result in special review and possibly financial penalties.

In the U.K., the NHS disseminates information on drug prices and notifies individual physicians when their prescribing costs exceed the norm for their specialty. Al-

---

of sales to the NHS + a per product allowance of roughly £41,000. The fixed amounts are indexed to the retail price index. Although this formula does not limit actual promotional expense, it limits the expense that can be deducted in calculating the ROC under the PPRS.

8. In countries with high prescription rates per capita such as Germany and Japan, the average physician visit takes three–five minutes.

though so far the drug budgets are only indicative for traditional GPs, whose capitation covers only their own services, they are expected to be made binding once the data are sufficiently detailed to reflect real differences in patient mix. In addition, under the 1989 NHS reforms, GPs can elect to become fundholders who are paid a capitation to cover a comprehensive range of ambulatory services including drugs. These fundholders face a direct financial incentive to limit drug spending, since they can retain half of any savings for investment in approved expenses of their practice.

Although physician drug budgets as adopted in Germany appear to achieve their goal of controlling drug spending, their effect on total costs is less clear and may indeed be perverse. Schulemberg and others (1994) report an increase in referrals by office-based physicians, who are subject to the budget caps, to hospitals that are not subject to the cap, with a general increase in total costs. More fundamentally, such crude budget limits lack the information that is necessary to accommodate the medical needs of specific patients. They create incentives for physicians to switch from more innovative but more costly drugs to older, less costly generic products, regardless of therapeutic appropriateness (Danzon and Liu 1996), and to avoid high-cost patients.

The Japanese System of Drug Reimbursement. The Japanese system incorporates both regulation and competition. A key feature of this system is that Japanese physicians generally dispense the drugs that they prescribe.[9] The government sets the reimbursement price for each drug. The dispensing physician or hospital receives this reimbursement from the social insurance program and, hence, profits directly from any margin between the reimbursement price and the manufacturer's price. Drug

---

9. South Korea uses a similar system.

manufacturers thus have incentives to cut their prices below the reimbursement price in order to increase the financial incentives of physicians to prescribe their drugs over those of their competitors. Every two years the government surveys the actual manufacturer prices charged and reduces the reimbursement price for those drugs for which the margin between the current reimbursement and the (weighted mean) manufacturer's price exceeds some "reasonable" zone, currently 13 percent.

This system successfully stimulates price reductions from manufacturers so that drug prices and government reimbursement prices fall in real terms over the life cycle of a drug. Between 1981 and 1992, real drug prices fell 7 percent a year in Japan (Danzon and Kim 1996). Japan, however, has among the highest number of scripts per capita, and drug spending as a percentage of total health spending is higher there than in other industrialized countries. Physicians derive roughly one-third of their income from prescribing. In addition to these distortions in incentives for the use of drugs, this system only passes on to payers and consumers any savings from manufacturer price cuts with a two-year lag, when reimbursement prices are revised downward.[10] Moreover, since manufacturers can obtain a price increase only by introducing a new product, this system creates incentives to focus R&D effort on producing a high volume of new products, even if they offer only marginal, if any, improvements over existing products. This incentive structure is widely blamed for the focus of Japanese R&D on minor product extensions, at least until recently.[11]

---

10. The Japanese government has unsuccessfully endorsed a policy of limiting physician dispensing (*bungyo*) for many years. A major obstacle to change is that, since profits from prescribing constitute a significant fraction of income for Japanese physicians and hospitals, fees for office visits and other medical services would have to be increased if provider incomes are to be maintained.

11. A bias toward minor extensions rather than truly innovative

Patient Copayments. Although many European countries
nominally include significant patient cost-sharing in their
social insurance programs, actual cost-sharing is often limited by supplementary insurance or exemptions. In
France, for example, although patient copayments under
the social security system nominally range up to 70 percent, depending on the class of drug, in practice only
roughly 3 percent of expenditures on reimbursable products are paid out of pocket because most people have
supplementary insurance that covers social security copayments.[12] Although the U.K. nominally has patient prescription charges, more than 80 percent of sales are
exempt because of exemptions for the elderly, needy, and
other categories. Copayment on physician visits, which is
a potentially significant component of the price to the patient of obtaining a prescription, is also typically low.
Moreover, insurance has traditionally covered an extensive range of drugs, including cold and cough remedies,
laxatives, and other preparations that U.S. consumers
typically purchase over the counter and without reimbursement. Given this extensive insurance, patient cost-
consciousness has not served as a constraint on demand
for drugs.

More recently, several countries have increased patient copayments. In 1993, Italy increased patient copayments, which had traditionally been low and had many
exemptions. A 50 percent copayment was applied for
drugs deemed marginally important, and many drugs
deemed inessential were made ineligible for reimbursement (delisted). Preliminary evidence suggests that this
increase in copayments has significantly reduced drug ex-

products need not necessarily occur if markups over existing products
are granted only to new products that represent a significant therapeutic advance. See Danzon and Zhang (1994).

12. An additional eleven percentage points of total pharmaceutical
spending are paid directly by consumers for nonreimbursable products
(SNIP 1993).

penditures in Italy, although the relative contributions of partial copayments and total delisting are not known. Although copayments in Germany were increased in 1993 to 3–7 marks, depending on the price of the drug, this is likely to be a minimal deterrent except for low-income patients or those on chronic medications.

The theory of optimal insurance implies that copayments should ideally be expressed as a percentage of the price, rather than a flat amount per script, and should be subject to an upper limit (stop-loss) that is lower for low-income persons and those on chronic medications, in order to provide appropriate financial protection. Since these two categories of users account for a significant fraction of drug expenditures, and these expenditures would thus be unconstrained once the stop-loss is reached, theory suggests that other controls are likely to remain a permanent part of insurance plans. The controls that are evolving under competing managed-care plans in the United States suggest the types of limits that consumers are willing to accept in return for lower drug costs.

Managed Care in the United States. In the United States, insurance coverage for outpatient drugs has traditionally been lower than for other ambulatory services. In 1994, about 50 percent of retail prescription drug expenditures was paid out of pocket (Gondek 1994). Prices were unregulated. Reimbursement under traditional insurance plans left great discretion to the prescribing physician in choice of drug.

Over the past decade, however, managed-care techniques have spread rapidly to pharmaceuticals, through health maintenance organizations and through specialty pharmacy benefit management companies that manage drug benefits for HMOs and for indemnity insurance plans. Hereafter, the term *pharmacy benefit managers* refers to both HMOs and specialized drug benefit managers. Strategies commonly used by PBMs include formularies of preferred drugs that may receive more comprehensive reimbursement; physician education and monitoring to channel use toward preferred drugs; and generic and therapeutic substitution in favor of generic and branded drugs for which discounts have been negotiated. This ability to move market share toward preferred drugs gives PBMs the leverage necessary to negotiate significant discounts from manufacturers. Similarly, PBMs contract with a selected network of pharmacies, negotiating discounts on dispensing fees in return for the increase in volume that accrues to members of the network. Mail order dispensing permits even greater control over the choice of drugs and dispensing margins.

The combination of discounts on branded drug prices, generic substitution, lower dispensing fees, and other administrative cost savings has enabled these PBMs to reduce drug expenditures by 30 percent or more in some plans. Drug utilization review systems offer a promising approach to improving quality through improved patient compliance and avoidance of adverse drug interactions. Moreover, since DUR uses on-line information systems, it can incorporate patient history and other information and, hence, be sensitive to real therapeutic needs, in contrast to the German physician drug budgets, which set physician-specific limits differentiated only by specialty.

4
Effects of Regulation on Drug Prices and Expenditures

How successful have price controls been in meeting their primary objective of controlling drug prices and expenditures? This chapter examines cross-country differences in price levels, volume of consumption per capita, the share of consumption devoted to global as opposed to minor compounds, and growth in expenditures. The evidence indicates that stringent price regulation, as enforced in France and Italy, has succeeded in holding down drug prices, on average, below prices in other countries. This "saving," however, has been more than offset by the growth in volume and upgrading of product mix, such that total drug spending per capita has continued to grow in real terms.

Price Indexes

To illustrate the differences in prices under alternative regulatory regimes, table 4–1 reports price indexes comparing manufacturer prices in eight countries relative to the United States for 1992. The indexes include all single-molecule products that are sold through outpatient pharmacies in both the United States and the foreign country under comparison.[1] We match products across countries

---

1. The data used here were provided by IMS International, under a grant from Pfizer Inc. to the University of Pennsylvania, for the study of international price comparisons for pharmaceuticals.

TABLE 4-1
PRICE INDEXES IN SELECTED COUNTRIES, RELATIVE TO THE UNITED STATES, 1992
(all single-molecule drugs, matched by MOL/ATC, outpatient pharmacy)

Country	Laspeyres-KG	Laspeyres-SU	Paasche-KG	Paasche-SU	N
United States	1.000	1.000	1.000	1.000	922
Canada	0.870	1.030	0.664	0.447	458
Germany	0.972	1.273	0.521	0.368	471
France	0.570	0.701	0.416	0.326	412
Italy	0.739	0.907	0.331	0.465	406
Japan	1.282	0.923	0.486	0.448	396
Switzerland	1.049	1.444	0.657	0.465	308
Sweden	0.811	1.089	0.566	0.370	261
United Kingdom	0.678	0.761	0.479	0.465	453

NOTES: Laspeyres = U.S. weights
　　　　Paasche = foreign weights
　　　　SU = price per standard unit
　　　　KG = price per kilogram
SOURCE: Danzon and Kim (1995), using IMS data.

31

if they have the same chemical composition (molecule) and are in the same anatomical therapeutic category (MOL/ATC), regardless of manufacturer or prescription status. This definition of matching products permits the most comprehensive sample possible in each country, including patented products that are sold under license to different manufacturers in different countries, and generic versions of off-patent products. Thus, whereas previous international price comparisons (for example, BEUC [1989]; GAO [1992, 1994a]) have been based on a small, unrepresentative sample of leading branded prescription drugs sold by the same originator company in all countries, the indexes reported here are as comprehensive as possible, including all versions of all matching compounds, regardless of manufacturer and prescription status.[2]

Here we report price indexes using two measures of price: price per standard unit and price per gram of active ingredient. A standard unit is defined as one tablet, one capsule, five milliliters of a liquid, etc., and is a rough proxy for a dose. Since the average strength per dose differs across countries, both for individual drugs and because of differences in the mix of drugs, however, comparisons based on price per dose and price per gram can differ substantially. These two measures of price permit us to include all dosage forms, strengths, and pack sizes for each product. Thus the price for each MOL/ATC is the weighted average price, averaged over all products in that MOL/ATC, and averaged over all packs and strengths. By contrast, previous studies have often compared only a single pack for each product, thereby restricting the comparison to a small and often unrepresentative

---

2. These indexes are not fully representative, since they necessarily omit drugs in each country that are not available in the other country. Drugs used in hospitals are also excluded, because price regulation typically applies only to outpatient sales. Hospital sales account for roughly 20–30 percent of total drug sales, and data are less complete.

sample of the sales for each drug in the sample, which is already an unrepresentative subset of all available drugs.[3] Here we forgo the requirement that matched drugs have the same manufacturer and same pack size and strength in order to include a much more representative sample of drugs than is possible if comparisons are restricted to drugs that are sold by the same manufacturer and in the same dosage form and strength in all countries.

Prices are at the manufacturer level, except that for the United States the reported prices overstate net prices received by manufacturers, because they do not reflect discounts, chargebacks, and rebates that are given to Medicaid, HMOs, and pharmacy benefit management programs. These indexes are therefore upward biased as a measure of net manufacturer prices in the United States relative to other countries. This upward bias is greater for brand prescription products than for generics or OTCs for which discounts are not the norm.

Table 4-1 compares price per standard unit and price per kilogram in eight countries—U.K., France, Germany, Italy, Canada, Sweden, Switzerland, and Japan—relative to the United States, using as weights either the U.S. consumption weights (Laspeyres indexes) or the foreign consumption weights (Paasche indexes). A value greater (less) than 1.00 implies that prices are higher (lower) in the foreign country than in the United States.[4]

In a comparison of price per standard unit, using the U.S. weights, France has the lowest prices relative to the United States (− 30 percent), followed by the U.K. (− 24 percent), Italy (− 9 percent), and Japan (− 8 percent). The other countries are more expensive than the United States, ranging from 3 percent more for Canada to 44 per-

---

3. Because packs and strengths differ across countries, even this single price must often be imputed, usually by linear interpolation from the most similar pack available.

4. A fuller analysis of these indexes is reported in Danzon and Kim (1995).

cent more for Switzerland. The indexes based on price per gram, however, generally show lower foreign prices relative to the United States. The appearance of lower foreign prices, when we compare price per gram rather than price per unit, results because average strength per dose is typically higher abroad than in the United States. The exception is Japan, which switches from being 8 percent less costly when price per standard unit is compared to 28 percent more expensive when price per gram is compared. This comparison reflects the relatively low strength per dose in Japan.

When we compare the Paasche indexes, which are based on the foreign country's consumption weights, then all countries appear cheaper than the United States. The pattern of relative prices remains: France, Italy, and the U.K. have the lowest prices relative to the United States, and Germany and Japan also drop. This finding, that foreign prices appear much lower when price indexes are based on foreign consumption weights, is a common phenomenon of price indexes for other industries and is known as the Gerschenkron effect. It results, in part, because all countries tend to use relatively more of the drugs that are relatively cheap in that country (Danzon and Chao 1996). This pattern is consistent with the standard laws of demand, that quantity demanded varies inversely with price. For drugs, it is also possible that regulators tend to impose particularly heavy price controls on drugs that have relatively high volume.

Price regulation falls hardest on patented, branded prescription (℞) drugs, which are the most innovative products and would hence command the highest prices. One side effect of these policies is to undermine competition from generic and over-the-counter (OTC) drugs, which thrive as a cheaper alternative to originator drugs in countries that permit more pricing freedom to originator drugs. The net effect is that the difference in the overall

FIGURE 4-1
PRICE PER STANDARD UNIT IN SELECTED COUNTRIES, RELATIVE TO THE UNITED STATES

Cost Relative to the United States

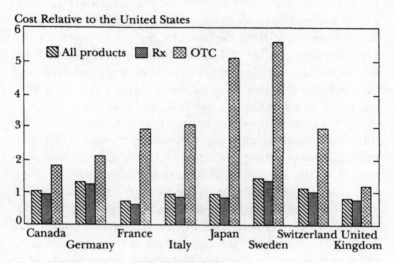

NOTE: MOL/ATC matching 1992 pharmacy.
SOURCE: Author's calculations, based on IMS data.

cost of drug therapy to consumers, including generics and OTCs, is not as great as appears from comparisons that focus exclusively on patented originator drugs.

To illustrate the bias that results from excluding generics and OTCs from international price comparisons, figure 4-1 shows Laspeyres price indexes based on price per standard unit for three categories: all drugs (as in table 4-1), branded ℞ drugs, and OTCs. Prices for brand ℞ products alone are higher in the United States than all comparison countries except Germany and Sweden. These conclusions change when generics and OTCs are included. For the total weighted average over all categories, Canada, Germany, Switzerland, and Sweden are more expensive than the United States, while France,

Italy, Japan, and the U.K. are less expensive. The changes are small for Germany and the U.K., which both have significant market shares of low-priced generics. The results for OTCs alone, however, are dramaticaly different: OTC prices are higher in all foreign markets than in the United States and more than 80 percent higher in seven of the eight foreign markets.[5] This finding is consistent with casual observation that the OTC market is more developed in the United States than in most foreign markets, with the possible exception of the U.K. and Canada.

This evidence demonstrates that conclusions on the difference in drug prices across countries can differ dramatically, depending on how the price indexes are constructed—the sample of drugs used, the measure of price (per dose or per gram), and the weights (domestic or foreign). For each country, the indexes based on its own consumption weights are plausibly most relevant, under the assumption that domestic consumption reflects local preferences and medical norms and would adapt slowly, if at all, if the price structure of another country were adopted. The use of purchasing power parities rather than exchange rates to convert to a common currency also makes a difference. Regardless of the measure used, prices in the two countries with heaviest regulation in 1992—France and Italy—are among the lowest of all comparison countries.[6]

---

5. Since we know Ŗ status only for the United States, the indexes labeled Ŗ include only Ŗ products for the U.S. sample, whereas foreign samples may include some OTC packs; the indexes labeled OTC include only OTC products for the United States, but the foreign samples may include some Ŗ products. Similarly, since generic status is known only for the United States, the indexes labeled brand-only may include some generic packs in other countries, which may bias down the estimates of brand prices abroad relative to the United States.

6. Although Germany had among the highest prices in 1992, these data do not show the effects of the stringent 1993 changes, so may overstate current price levels in Germany.

Given these low manufacturer price levels in France, the theory developed below implies that price regulation has adversely affected the incentives and ability of French firms to invest in innovative R&D. Moreover, this evidence also establishes the important potential impact that price regulation in one country can have on prices in other countries and on total revenues for global products if these low prices are exported through parallel trade or international price comparisons.

The results also suggest that conclusions about overall effects of regulatory regimes cannot be based on comparison of prices for originator ℞ products only. The market share and pricing of generics and OTCs depend on the prices of the pioneer brand and on the price elasticity of demand and extent of competition in the market. Price regulation tends to undermine price competition and incentives for entry of generics and OTCs (Danzon and Chao 1996). In Japan, for example, where regulation reduces brand prices in real terms over the life-cycle, generics account for only 3–7 percent of drug sales (Ikegami 1995), compared with 30 percent or more of scripts in the United States, the U.K., and Germany. This bias in price comparisons and inferences about the effects of regulation will increase as the market share of generics and OTCs grows in the United States, Canada, Germany, and the U.K., as patents expire on a large number of leading products, and as private and public payers increasingly reimburse only at generic price levels.

Growth in Drug Expenditures

Despite the success of regulation in holding down prices, this has not carried through to control of total drug spending. Table 4–2 compares the growth in real per capita expenditures on drugs in five countries with different regulatory regimes for the period 1970–1990, adjusted for inflation using each country's own GDP deflator. France

TABLE 4–2
GROWTH IN REAL PER CAPITA EXPENDITURES ON PHARMACEUTICALS
IN SELECTED COUNTRIES, 1970–1990
(1980 = 100)

Country	1970	1975	1980	1985	1990
France	87.1	100.5	100	119.8	146.3
Germany	56.6	81.1	100	115.7	135.1
Italy	60.8	72.8	100	139.4	189.9
United Kingdom	na	86.7	100	110.9	126.0[a]
United States	90.9	91.8	100	121	144.8

a. 1989 data for U.K.
SOURCE: OECD health data, April 1993.

and Italy illustrate countries with price regulation; the
U.K. has profit regulation; Germany and the United States
had free pricing before 1989, when Germany introduced
reference pricing and the United States imposed Medicaid rebates.

Since 1980, real spending per capita has grown most
rapidly in Italy (90 percent), followed by France (46 percent), the United States (45 percent), and Germany (35
percent), with the U.K. lagging last (26 percent). For the
1970s, Germany grew most rapidly (43 percent), followed
by Italy (39 percent) and France (13 percent) with the
United States lagging (8 percent) (U.K. data not available). Interestingly, expenditure growth in Germany
slowed in the first half of the 1980s, even before the introduction of reference pricing in 1989.[7]

These data clearly demonstrate that regulation of
manufacturer prices is neither necessary nor sufficient to
control growth in total drug expenditures.[8] This is not sur-

---

7. Since reference pricing was phased in slowly, these data through
1990 are too recent to show the full long-term effects of the reference
price system when fully implemented or the effects of Germany's 1993
drug budgets and price controls. See Danzon and Liu (1996).

8. Since the expenditure data are at retail levels, the prices reflect
markups for wholesale and retail distribution margins and value-added

prising since drug expenditures depend on the volume and mix of drugs purchased per capita in addition to prices. The volume and mix of drugs depend on the extent of insurance coverage, on the associated consumer cost-sharing, which was minimal in France, Italy, and Germany for the period 1970–1990, and on physician reimbursement and medical norms. In general, drug use appears to be greater and has grown most rapidly in countries where physicians are reimbursed fee-for-service (France, Japan, Germany), compared with countries such as the U.K., where physicians receive a fixed capitation payment per enrollee per month.[9] This effect of physician reimbursement on drug use is plausible: if patients are fully insured, the physician who is reimbursed fee-for-service has a financial incentive to prescribe the best available drugs to patients and to require frequent return visits to refill prescriptions, as a means of competing for and generating reimbursable visits. Thus, on the one hand, the design of the insurance system reflects medical norms and provider interests; on the other hand, insurance design influences medical practice patterns, including the use of drugs.

Volume per Capita

To illustrate the differences in volume and growth of drug consumption per capita, table 4–3 reports estimates of drug consumption relative to the United States, obtained

taxes (VAT), in addition to manufacturer prices. The regulation of these margins in countries with price controls eliminates the price competition at the retail level that prevails in countries with unregulated pharmacy sectors, such as the United States. This lack of competition at the retail pharmacy level may also contribute to the higher prices and lower prevalence of OTCs in countries that regulate prices for prescription drugs.

9. In Italy, capitation of primary care physicians recently replaced fee-for-service reimbursement.

TABLE 4-3
DRUG VOLUME PER CAPITA IN SELECTED COUNTRIES, 1981–1990
(real quantities relative to United States = 100)

Country	1981	1982	1983	1984	1985	1986	1987	1988	1989	1990
France	222.2	208.2	206.7	218.5	211.1	256.8	301.6	331.8	356.4	396.7
Germany	152.2	147.4	149.1	154.9	149.1	192.9	221.2	221.9	233.1	277.4
Italy	124.0	143.0	135.0	139.3	142.1	171.8	213.5	213.5	239.3	286.3
United Kingdom	61.0	64.1	63.9	63.4	60.5	68.5	71.9	73.6	74.9	na
United States	100	100	100	100	100	100	100	100	100	100

NOTE: See footnote 10.
SOURCE: See Danzon and Percy (1996).

by dividing the ratio of drug expenditures by an index of relative prices.[10] These estimates indicate that real drug consumption in France is almost 300 percent higher than in the United States; Italy and Germany are more than 150 percent higher; and the U.K. is 25 percent below the United States. These differentials between other countries and the United States have increased over time, possibly reflecting the higher copayments in the United States.

Since these estimates of consumption volumes per capita reflect the total number of units or doses, it is important to note that the mix of drugs differs greatly cross-nationally. The high consumption volumes in France, Italy, and Germany partly reflect a relatively high consumption of minor compounds that are not marketed in the United States (we return to this below). The point here is that since the mix of drugs in any country is fairly stable over time, the evidence in table 4–3 demonstrates that regulation has not controlled growth in volume. Relative to the United States, which has had free pricing but significant copayments, volume has grown most rapidly in Italy (131 percent) and France (79 percent), the countries with the heaviest regulation of prices; volume has grown rapidly in Germany (82 percent), which had free pricing for most of the period but minimal copayment; volume has grown relatively slowly in the U.K. (23 percent), which had profit regulation but no direct price controls.

Mix of Drugs

To illustrate differences in the mix of drugs consumed and the importance of local products in certain coun-

10. The price index used is the average of the Fisher indexes for price per gram and price per standard unit. Each Fisher index is a geometric mean of the Laspeyres and Paasche indexes, which use U.S. and foreign weights, respectively.

tries,[11] table 4–4 compares the markets for single-molecule cardiovascular products in these nine major pharmaceutical markets. The United States has the greatest number of individual products (710), which is not surprising given its larger population. Although Germany's population was roughly one-fifth that of the United States, Germany has only 13 percent fewer products (619); Japan is third (449). Germany ranks first in number of molecules (198), followed by Japan (158), Italy (154), France (150), and the United States (105). These data strongly suggest that the relatively high drug consumption volumes in France, Italy, and Germany, compared with the United States (see table 4–3), partly reflect their large number of compounds (molecules), including many that are not sold in the United States. The number of products per molecule, however, is highest in the United States, reflecting the greater number of generic substitutes per molecule.[12]

The second and third panels in table 4–4 show the percentage of each country's market that is accounted for by molecules that are available in both the United States and the comparison country. The share of each market that is devoted to drugs that are available in the United States can be interpreted as a rough indicator of the market share of drugs of relatively high therapeutic value.[13] The United States is the most attractive market to enter because it is the largest and has relatively high prices; the

---

11. These data are discussed in more detail in Danzon and Kim (1995).

12. The number of products per molecule includes licensed comarketed versions of the originator product as well as generics. Comarketing is common, often under regulatory pressure, in France and Italy.

13. The number of major markets in the world in which a particular drug is available is a widely used measure of therapeutic value since innovator firms generally attempt to market a drug in any market where the expected revenues cover the incremental costs of launch in that country. The number of markets of penetration is not available to us.

TABLE 4–4
MARKETS FOR SINGLE-MOLECULE CARDIOVASCULAR PRODUCTS (OUTPATIENT PHARMACY), IN SELECTED COUNTRIES, 1992

	United States	Canada	Germany	France	Italy	Japan	United Kingdom	Switzerland	Sweden
Number of products									
Local products	710	157	619	263	365	449	176	160	109
Molecules	105	66	198	150	154	158	93	97	60
Products per molecule	6.76	2.38	3.13	1.75	2.37	2.84	1.89	1.65	1.98
% of molecules available in both countries									
U.S. molecules, % match		50	61	51	54	56	59	43	41
Foreign molecules, % match		79	32	36	37	37	67	46	72
% of sales on matching molecules									
U.S. sales, % match		94	96	95	97	95	96	91	76
Foreign sales, % match		97	61	47	58	57	89	74	92

SOURCE: Danzon and Kim (1996); IMS data.

FDA standards of safety and efficacy, however, are generally considered the most stringent of all major markets. Firms generally attempt to launch in the United States any product that has sufficient therapeutic value to satisfy FDA requirements for safety and efficacy and sufficient economic value to justify the costs of launch, including filing for FDA approval. Thus, availability in the United States is a rough indicator of therapeutic value.

The percentage of sales accounted for by molecules that are available in the United States is lowest in France (47 percent), with Japan (57 percent) and Italy (58 percent) next lowest. By contrast, in the U.K., these U.S.-matching molecules account for 89 percent of sales. More than 90 percent of cardiovascular sales in the United States is molecules that have penetrated each of the other eight markets, except for Sweden (76 percent), which is a relatively small market.

Using availability in the United States as an indicator of therapeutic value, these data suggest that more than half of the cardiovascular sales in France is on products that either could not meet FDA standards for safety and efficacy or had insufficient economic value to cover the costs of launch in the United States. This evidence on consumption patterns supports the hypothesis, developed further below, that the price regulatory system in France has diverted R&D toward imitative rather than innovative products. France has fairly lax regulatory requirements for proof of efficacy (Thomas 1993), which permit these products to reach the French market whereas most would almost certainly not survive the FDA screen. Supported by generous insurance reimbursement, these minor products account for roughly half of total drug expenditures in the cardiovascular category. Since at higher price levels more innovative products would be relatively more profitable, a tentative conclusion is that price regulation is a necessary condition (if not a sufficient condition) for this diversion of consumption to minor products. By contrast, in the U.K., which is the leading innovator country after the United States and has similarly high regulatory standards, U.S.-available drugs account for 89 percent of sales.

Conclusion

The evidence confirms that stringent price regulation, as adopted in France and Italy, has been successful at holding down prices of originator prescription drugs, relative to levels in other major markets with freer pricing. Despite low prices, expenditures have grown at least as rapidly under these regulatory regimes as in other countries with less aggressive controls because of growth of volume and upgrading of the mix of drugs. Moreover, price controls have other indirect effects. Regulation tends to undermine competition such that countries with heavier regulation have less competition from generic and over-the-counter drugs, which thrive as cheaper alternatives in countries that permit freer pricing of branded prescription drugs.

The net effect is that the overall difference in the price of drug therapy to consumers, between heavily regulated markets, such as France and Italy, and those that permit freer pricing, such as the United States and Germany pre-1989, is not as great as has been argued in studies that compare only the prices of the leading, brand-name drugs (for example, GAO [1993, 1994a]). At the same time, price regulation appears to sustain a large market share of domestically produced, minor compounds that lack proven therapeutic merit but that nevertheless absorb more than one-third of total drug spending in some countries. Thus regulation appears to distort drug consumption and hence value for money for consumers, as well as costs to regulators and returns to manufacturers.

5
Effects of Regulation on Innovation

The primary goal of drug price regulation is to reduce drug expenditures by payers. Since the price paid by payers is the average revenue to drug manufacturers (after adjusting for copayments and distribution margins), regulation that reduces prices tends to reduce manufacturer average revenue per unit and hence reduce incentives for R&D. Total R&D spending can be broadly categorized into two types: R&D investment that is targeted at the discovery of truly new therapies or significant improvements in old therapies (hereafter "innovative" R&D) and R&D investment that merely attempts minor modifications of existing molecules, new dosage forms, and line extensions (hereafter "imitative" R&D). The different forms of regulation have different effects on incentives to allocate R&D to these different forms of innovation. Moreover, regulation also affects R&D spending indirectly through effects on the cost of capital.

This chapter describes the incentive effects on R&D of the main forms of regulation described in chapter 3. We focus on the incentive to engage in innovative versus imitative R&D. Initially, we assume a closed economy, in which each firm produces only for its domestic market. In reality, certain effects of each country's regulation do fall most heavily on its domestic firms, particularly on those with minimal sales and investments abroad. In addition, however, each country's regulation affects the subsidiaries of multinational firms selling global drugs in that country.

Regulatory systems may also have spillover interactions with foreign markets through parallel trade and international price comparisons. These global effects are considered in chapter 7.

Innovation Strategies of the Pharmaceutical Firm

The effects of alternative forms of regulation on incentives for innovative R&D can be analyzed using a formal model of a pharmaceutical firm's decision to allocate its R&D budget toward investments that target innovative rather than imitative products.[1] In reality, such targeting is highly uncertain—firm A's investments to develop a new compound may intend to be innovative when initiated, only to prove imitative when completed many years later because firms B and C have beaten firm A in the R&D race. Moreover, the true potential of compounds is sometimes discovered through serendipity, only after years of use for other purposes. The first successful AIDS drug, acyclovir, for example, was initially developed in the 1960s for other purposes, and its potential for treating AIDS was discovered only in the 1980s. Nevertheless, while great uncertainty applies to the ex post success of individual compounds, there are clear ex ante distinctions between R&D strategies that target and have the potential for truly innovative discoveries, only some of which may ultimately succeed, and R&D strategies that aim only at minor modifications and so have no chance of producing major innovative breakthroughs.

The firm's decision to target innovative rather than imitative products involves a trade-off between expected revenues and costs. In the absence of regulatory constraints, innovative products can expect to realize higher prices or larger volumes than imitative products. Conversely, investing in innovative products entails greater

---

1. The formal model is described in Danzon and Zhang (1994).

risks and costs. The safety and efficacy profiles of new substances are less predictable than for imitative products,
which have known modes of action and interaction. For a
given probability of passing regulatory screens for safety
and efficacy, innovative products often entail higher R&D
costs, for example, because larger and longer clinical trials may be required to assure statistically significant effects
with unknown compounds.[2]

The analysis here assumes that a pharmaceutical firm
selects a target or expected degree of innovativeness for
its R&D budget, given this structure of expected risks, revenues, and costs. The firm will target more innovative
products that entail greater risk of failure or higher R&D
costs only if the expected revenues are sufficiently high to
offset these higher costs. Formally, the firm's optimal
R&D strategy balances the higher costs and higher risks
(lower probability of regulatory approval) of targeting
more innovative products against their higher expected
revenue.[3] In general, the larger the size of the potential
market, the more innovative is the optimal R&D portfolio
because a high volume permits broader spreading of the
fixed costs of innovative R&D.

Rather than examine each country's regulation in detail, we focus on certain prototypes or basic characteristics
of the regulatory systems described earlier and show how
these characteristics affect a pharmaceutical firm's optimal R&D strategy. In the following sections, we discuss

---

2. The analysis requires only that these assumptions hold true on
average, not necessarily for every innovative product. Giving some innovative products priority in the regulatory review process, for example, would reduce the delay component of costs for innovative drugs.
Similarly, the analysis does not require that all innovative products
have absolutely high prices, only that consumers and payers would pay
more for innovative products than for imitative products in the same
therapeutic class, in the absence of regulation.

3. The analysis abstracts from the heterogeneous expertise and resources of different firms to focus on the common influence of regulation incentives.

the direct revenue effects of regulation and the indirect effects, through the cost of capital; differential effects on domestic and foreign firms; and empirical evidence.

Revenue Effects of Regulation

Proportional Price Regulation. Proportional price regulation reduces prices for all products by the same percentage, relative to their unconstrained, free market level. Such proportional price cuts would occur under a system of regulation based on international price comparisons, for example, if country A sets its prices based on country B whose prices are systematically lower than prices in country A in the absence of regulation.

Proportional price regulation creates incentives for the pharmaceutical firm to target its research at less innovative products because at lower price levels, expected revenues are insufficient to cover the higher costs and greater risks of innovative products. The negative impact is expected to be greatest for products that target indications that affect relatively few patients.

Biased Price Regulation. In practice, most forms of price and reimbursement regulation are biased: they tend to impose a larger percentage price cut on more innovative products than on imitative products. Regulation that imposes proportionately greater price cuts on innovative products has an even more negative effect on incentives for innovation than proportional regulation that applies the same percentage price cut to all products.

The most basic reason for regulatory bias against innovative products is that regulators whose aim is to control drug expenditures focus disproportionately on products that have relatively high prices or volumes, since these products tend to account for a disproportionate share of expenditures. These obvious targets, however, also tend to be the more innovative drugs. France, for example, applied its *envelope globale*, whereby prices are reduced to offset unexpectedly large volume increases, only to major drugs.

A second characteristic of price regulation that is likely to introduce systematic bias against innovative products is internal comparison to prices of existing products as a benchmark for setting new product prices. Regulation based on internal comparison is particularly harmful to innovation in countries whose regulatory systems do not permit routine inflation adjustments, such that prices of old products fall in real value over time. By contrast, the costs of R&D have been rising in real terms over time. If regulation based on internal comparisons does not permit prices for new products to reflect both inflation and any increase in real R&D costs in excess of inflation, such regulation will tend to be systematically biased against innovative products.

Third, reference price reimbursement as implemented in Germany, the Netherlands, and New Zealand is systematically biased against innovative new drugs if they are grouped with and therefore reimbursed at the same prices as existing products. The single "reference" or reimbursement price for a group acts as a ceiling on the price that manufacturers can effectively charge. This single price imposes the largest price cut on those drugs in the group that would otherwise command the highest prices, which tend to be the most innovative drugs.

The differing detail of reference price systems affects the extent of their adverse impact on innovation. If reference pricing applies only to generic substitutes (as in Phase 1 in Germany), then differential returns to innovation can still be realized as long as a drug is on patent, but these are eliminated when the patent expires and generic substitutes become available. If reference pricing includes in a single group both old and newer, improved versions of a drug or class—such as a once-a-day, delayed-release form and short-acting forms—then there is no incentive for manufacturers to develop improved forms of existing products. At the extreme, if reference pricing groups are broadly defined to apply to therapeutic substitutes (somehow defined), including drugs that differ in chemical composition and some drugs that are still on patent, then returns to innovative R&D may be entirely eliminated. By setting a single price for old and new drugs, such broad reference pricing undermines the value of patents to manufacturers and nullifies the policy purpose of patent protection.[4]

Regulators may be aware of the adverse effects of regulation on incentives for innovation and may nominally attempt to manipulate the structure of regulated prices to award higher prices for innovative products while cutting average prices. In theory, regulatory bias could be designed to favor rather than penalize innovative products. In practice, however, regulators are unlikely to have the information or the incentive to design the regulatory price structure such that it promotes innovation. Consistent with this, France and Japan in theory grant higher percentage price increases over existing products for innovative new drugs. Both casual evidence and the more formal evidence presented below, however, suggest that the regulatory systems in both France and Japan have, in fact, diverted the R&D of these countries' domestic firms toward developing many minor modifications of old drugs rather than fewer, more innovative new products. Regulation rewards virtually any new drug with a higher price, almost without regard to its innovative merit. The lower the permitted price differential for innovation, the more likely it is that an imitative strategy of developing many

---

4. In theory, regulators may permit exemptions from reference pricing for products that they consider truly innovative. Such discretion at minimum adds uncertainty; in practice, it is also likely to be systematically biased against innovation because of pressures on regulators to control drug spending. Since 1995, on-patent drugs are excluded from reference pricing in Germany to preserve incentives for innovation.

minor compounds dominates a more innovative strategy of targeting fewer, major compounds. Moreover, in both of these countries, this tendency for price regulation to encourage imitation is reinforced by relatively low regulatory requirements for efficacy, which reduce the risk of regulatory rejection for minor compounds.

Company-specific Revenue Constraints. In 1994, France introduced a new control system of company-specific revenue constraints. This system was to set a cap on revenue growth for each company as a means of constraining the government's total drug spending growth to a target level, such as 3 percent a year.

In theory, these revenue limits could be differentiated across companies to reward firms that pursue innovative strategies and to penalize firms that merely develop imitative and minor new products. In practice, political pressures are likely to be strong for uniform growth targets for all companies. Even in the absence of political pressures, governments are unlikely to have the information required to adopt different revenue limits for different companies that appropriately reward the development of innovative products. In principle, cost-effectiveness and cost-benefit techniques offer a framework that regulators might use to place rough values on alternative drugs and hence to permit higher revenue growth for firms that develop innovative products. In practice, these tools are rough and cannot be expected to yield precise and timely answers to all the questions that regulators must address if firm-specific revenue caps are to encourage or, at least, remain neutral rather than discourage innovation.

If growth targets are, in fact, virtually uniform across companies, the effect will be to discourage R&D that would lead to revenue growth in excess of the target. In particular, a uniform limit would discourage innovative R&D relative to imitative R&D. With a uniform revenue limit the firm that incurs higher costs of innovative R&D could not earn commensurably higher revenues to cover the higher costs. Indeed, the rational response of a firm faced with a fixed revenue constraint is to invest the minimum in R&D necessary to achieve the permitted revenue cap. If innovative R&D entails costs in excess of this minimum necessary to achieve the revenue cap, such innovative R&D will be shunned in favor of me-too products that entail lower costs. Thus, although revenue growth constraints that are uniform across companies may have some appearance of objectivity, in fact they are biased against companies that invest in innovation.

Profit Regulation. Under the pharmaceutical profit regulation system (PPRS) in the United Kingdom, the government permits a firm-specific rate of return on capital (ROC) that depends on such factors as innovation and other contributions to the U.K. economy. Several features make this profit regulation system more favorable to innovation than France's or Italy's price regulation system or Germany's reference price system and drug budgets.

The U.K. controls apply to the rate of return on capital, including investments in R&D, rather than to individual prices or total gross revenues. As long as the allowed rate of return is at least equal to the appropriate risk-adjusted return required by equity markets, firms have an incentive to invest in innovative products, even if these require greater capital outlays than imitative products. The system ensures that revenues will rise sufficiently to yield the permitted return on the higher capital investments required for innovation. Indeed, because companies with innovative portfolios are also permitted to earn a higher rate of return on capital, the higher risk of pursuing an innovative strategy is in principle rewarded. Whether this additional reward for risk in reality exceeds or falls short of the rewards for risk that are required by equity markets is an open question.

The U.K. system also entails lower administrative costs and risks for manufacturers than systems of direct price regulation. By permitting free pricing of new products, for example, the U.K. system reduces uncertainty and delay in launch compared with countries such as France that require regulatory approval of price before a new product can be reimbursed. In addition, the five-year life of the PPRS agreement, the three-year targets for allowable R&D expenditure, the formulas for allowable promotion expense, and other features reduce uncertainty for manufacturers and facilitate long-term planning. Certainly, the U.K.'s limit on ROC is likely to be less harmful to innovation than France's limit on revenue growth since an ROC limit automatically permits revenue to grow in proportion to R&D investments. By contrast, a gross revenue limit that ignores capital costs imposes a lower ROC for firms that invest more in innovative R&D, unless regulators are extremely skillful and politically courageous in differentiating revenue targets across companies to reward innovation.

The 1993 revisions of the PPRS, however, threaten to undermine its traditionally favorable incentives for innovation. These unfavorable changes include price cuts and a price freeze; a reduction in the gray area—the permitted deviation of actual from target ROC—from 50 percent to 25 percent; limits on allowable promotional expense for new drugs; and a requirement for rebates to the NHS if sales in any of the first five years after launch exceed £5 million. All these changes hit particularly hard at potential blockbuster new drugs and are expected to adversely affect incentives for innovation. Unfortunately, the full effects of these changes on the rate of innovation will not be manifest for many years. Moreover, because U.K. firms participate heavily in global markets, any effect of the U.K. environment on their incentives for innovation is masked by the effects of changes occurring simultaneously in other countries.

Physician Drug Budgets. Placing the physician at risk for the cost of drugs, as implemented in Germany in 1993, creates incentives for physicians to reduce their prescriptions of costly drugs, with substitution where necessary of cheaper and often inferior drugs. These financial incentives may, in theory, be constrained by professional norms and altruistic concern for patients. Market forces can also work if patients are sufficiently well informed and are willing to switch from physicians who prescribe the cheapest drug when a more effective drug for the patient's condition is available, albeit at a higher price. In practice, however, patients' information and willingness to switch have apparently been insufficient to counteract effectively physicians' financial incentives to choose the least costly drug rather than either the most effective or the most cost-effective.

In Germany, in the first six months of the 1993 physician drug budgets, total drug spending was almost 17 percent below the permissible 1991 ceiling (Schulemberg et al. 1993), which implies an even larger percentage cut relative to 1992 spending.[5] The longer-term evidence through 1994 confirms that placing physicians at financial risk for the cost of drugs has led to fewer prescriptions and to substitution of cheaper products, including generics and older drugs, for newer drugs that have higher prices (Danzon and Liu 1996). Similarly, when a strict cap on prescribing costs was imposed in the U.K., innovative and hence more expensive medicines tended to be prescribed much less frequently.[6]

Because physician drug budgets have the greatest impact on expensive drugs, they are likely to have severe adverse effects on incentives for innovation. These adverse

---

5. The rate of referrals to other physicians and hospital admissions simultaneously increased, plausibly to obtain access to inpatient drugs that were not subject to the cap (Schulemberg et al. 1993).

6. Striegler (1992), cited in Schulemberg et al. (1993).

effects of physician drug budgets on the use of costly drugs may in theory be mitigated to the extent that the allowed budgets are differentiated among physicians to reflect the individual needs of their panel of patients. In practice, however, such adjustments are likely to remain crude.

Effects of Regulation on the Cost of Capital

In addition to the direct revenue effects of price regulation just described, a second channel through which price regulation adversely affects innovation is raising the cost of capital. R&D in large pharmaceutical firms is funded almost exclusively from retained earnings. This pattern strongly suggests that retained earnings provide a lower cost source of capital than external financing for R&D, plausibly because of asymmetric information in equity markets.[7] Hence, if retained earnings are the least costly form of financing for R&D, regulation that reduces revenues and hence the flow of retained earnings raises the cost of R&D. This impact is greater for innovative R&D, which requires greater research investments, than for imitative R&D. Thus, regulation that reduces the revenues of research-based pharmaceutical firms has a double-barreled effect on innovative R&D: the direct effect of lower expected revenues and the indirect effect through the higher cost of capital.

Effects on Domestic and Foreign Firms

Although pharmaceutical markets are global—an innovative product can be sold in most major markets of the world—nevertheless, stringent domestic price regulation

---

7. See, for example, Myers and Majluf (1984). Equity markets may infer bad news when an established firm attempts to raise external equity. Such an inference does not apply to external funding raised by start-up firms, notably biotech firms, because they lack established products to generate a flow of retained earnings.

is likely to have the greatest adverse effect on the innovative ability of domestic firms, for several reasons. Domestic firms tend to have a disproportionate share of their home market. U.S.-based firms, for example, earn roughly 50 percent of their revenues in the U.S. market, although the United States accounts for only 30 percent of the world market. Thus, a cut in prices in the U.S. market would imply a larger percentage cut in total revenues for U.S. firms than for U.K. or German firms that earn a larger share of their revenues in European markets.

Conversely, foreign firms are likely to face higher costs and other disadvantages relative to the domestic firms in any market. These hurdles for foreign firms include information disadvantages in regulatory and other areas; unfamiliarity with and outright bias in medical markets (physicians and consumers may prefer products made by domestic firms with more local reputational capital); and costs of repatriating funds from the foreign market. Small foreign firms seek to reduce these costs by entering a local market through outlicensing of their products to firms based in the local market. Selling abroad through outlicensing, however, yields lower net returns to the originator firm than direct marketing does, as evidenced by the fact that, as pharmaceutical firms grow, they invariably establish their own subsidiaries in all major foreign markets.

These cost and information disadvantages of selling abroad imply a double bind for firms that are based in a country with low prices and are seeking to become innovative, multinational companies with global products. Most of their revenues derives from their home market. But the low prices in this domestic market yield insufficient retained earnings both to invest in innovative R&D and to establish subsidiaries in foreign markets where they could earn greater revenues. Consistent with this situation, as regulation has become more stringent in France and Japan, the major firms in these countries are seeking to establish their own base in the United States, through acquisition of U.S.-based firms, joint ventures, and other strategies. All of these strategies are slow and costly; whether they will enable the foreign firms to develop and maintain strong research-based programs remains to be seen.

Empirical Evidence

The effects of different regulatory systems on drug innovation are hard to measure precisely because of the long lags in the R&D process and because innovative success depends on many factors, in addition to regulation. Nevertheless, the available evidence is consistent with the prediction that regulation adversely affects innovation.

R&D Spending. Figure 5–1 shows trends in real (inflation-adjusted) R&D spending on ethical (prescription-bound) pharmaceuticals over the period 1981–1991.[8] The data reported for each country include all R&D spending in that country by foreign-based as well as domestic companies. Since multinational firms tend to perform most of their R&D in their home country, however, the reported spending in each country is heavily influenced by the R&D spending of that country's domestic firms.

These data indicate that the growth in R&D spending has been most rapid in the United States. The relative ranking of the other countries differs over the period, with acceleration in Japan and an apparent downturn in

---

8. The R&D data, unadjusted for inflation, are from a survey of the pharmaceutical trade associations in each country conducted by Centre for Medicines Research (1993). The data for France, Italy, and Japan are upward biased because they include equipment and land, which are excluded for the other countries; growth rates, however, should be unbiased, assuming that the share of capital in total expenditures is constant over the period.

FIGURE 5–1
GROWTH IN REAL R&D EXPENDITURES IN SELECTED COUNTRIES, 1981–1991

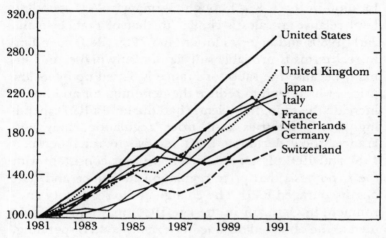

NOTE: Adjusted using GDP deflator.
SOURCE: Author's calculations using data from Centre for Medicines Research (1993).

France in most recent years. Germany grew rapidly through 1986 but then slowed considerably. How far this change reflects anticipation of Germany's progressively tighter price and volume controls or other factors such as labor costs and tax considerations cannot be determined from the available data. Also unknown is whether German pharmaceuticals firms have reduced their total R&D spending growth or have simply allocated a larger fraction to other countries, such as the United States and Japan, to achieve more closely matched currency flows of revenues and expenditures.

Table 5–1 shows R&D expenditures as a percentage of total spending on pharmaceuticals, for each country compared with the United States. R&D relative to sales in the U.K. is more than twice as high as in any other country, consistent with the hypothesis that rate-of-return regulation in the U.K. has encouraged R&D—or at least its location in the U.K. Although Germany's R&D spending level relative to sales is similar to that of France in the early 1980s and appears lower after 1986, R&D spending in real terms is probably still significantly higher in Germany because the ratio for France is biased up by its low prices, which tend to reduce the denominator and hence increase the ratio. Italy clearly had the lowest R&D spending. Both countries with price regulation, Italy and France, show declining R&D relative to sales between 1981 and 1991. These R&D data are thus consistent with the hypothesis that price regulation in France and Italy has discouraged R&D. The change in the regulatory environment in Germany in the late 1980s may have contributed to the observed decline in Germany's R&D spending. These conclusions on effects of regulation on R&D spending are tentative, however, in the absence of controls for other factors that may influence R&D.

Number of Innovations. Although these figures on total R&D spending are suggestive, they make no distinction between expenditures on innovative and expenditures on imitative R&D. Regulatory systems that automatically reward new products with higher prices, without differentiation between innovative and imitative products, may encourage high R&D spending but mostly in imitative, minor compounds rather than true innovation.

The evidence on the development of innovative products in different countries is consistent with this bias being particularly severe in France and Japan. Barral (1990, 1995) reports the number of new drugs discovered by different countries, categorized by degree of globalization and innovation. Of the 1,061 new drugs developed over the twenty-year period 1975–1994, 152 are global, de-

TABLE 5-1

R&D Share of Sales in Selected Countries, relative to the United States, 1981–1991

Country	1981	1982	1983	1984	1985	1986	1987	1988	1989	1990	1991
France	98.8	99.2	102.0	105.2	105.2	99.7	103.9	92.6	91.8	92.5	81.3
Germany	94.7	91.9	98.9	106.0	114.2	109.0	91.7	74.0	77.1	75.5	—
Italy	90.2	77.4	72.0	69.0	65.0	62.7	59.6	60.3	63.1	60.0	—
United Kingdom	204.4	187.0	196.2	208.6	217.6	217.3	190.1	199.6	205.8	—	—
United States	100.0	100.0	100.0	100.0	100.0	100.0	100.0	100.0	100.0	100.0	100.0

Sources: R&D data from Centre for Medicines Research (1993). Pharmaceutical expenditures from OECD Health.

fined as marketed in seven major markets; 273 are international, defined as marketed in four of the seven major markets; the remaining 636 are noninternational, defined as marketed in fewer than four major markets. New drugs are also categorized according to a medical evaluation of whether they offer a significant therapeutic improvement or employ a new chemical structure. Of the 1,061 new drugs, 109 are rated A (therapeutic improvement and new chemical structure); 219 are rated B (therapeutic improvement, known chemical structure); 150 are rated C (no therapeutic improvement, new chemical structure); and 583 are rated D (neither therapeutically nor chemically innovative.) Thus the majority of new drugs are neither global nor innovative: only 10–15 percent can be categorized as offering major therapeutic advance or achieving global penetration.

The discovery of global products is concentrated in three countries—the United States (45 percent), the United Kingdom (14 percent), and Switzerland (8 percent)—with all other countries combined contributing the remaining 33 percent. Although France ranks third in number of new chemical entities introduced between 1975 and 1989, after the United States and Japan, it ranks seventh in terms of "internationalized" products (launched in at least four of the seven major pharmaceutical markets) and eighth in terms of global products (launched in all seven major markets), after much smaller countries including Belgium, Switzerland, and Sweden (SNIP 1993). France and Italy have produced no global products since 1985; in 1993, only one French product appeared in the list of the top 100 global products, ranked by global sales.[9]

Particularly significant is the lack of penetration of French products in North American markets. Only 6.8 percent of French pharmaceutical exports were to North

---

9. Medical Ad News Supplement (1993).

America, which accounts for one-third of total world sales; this figure contrasts with 16.7 percent of U.K. exports and 15.0 percent of Swiss sales destined for North America. Sales by French companies account for only 1.2 percent of the U.S. market and 0.2 percent of the Japanese market; by contrast, German firms account for 4.6 percent and 4.8 percent of sales in the United States and Japan, respectively, and U.K. firms account for 14.6 percent and 2.9 percent (SNIP 1993). Similarly, sales by French firms are a smaller percentage of total sales in the major European markets than sales by German and U.K. firms.[10] Japan has produced 241 new products over the twenty-year period, compared with 59 for the U.K.; but only 3 percent of Japanese drugs are rated A and 69 percent are rated D, whereas 12 percent of U.K. drugs are rated A, and only 41 percent rated D.

Conclusions

Theoretical analysis shows that price regulation is likely to reduce innovation because of both lower expected revenues and a higher cost of capital. Although the effects of regulation in a single country are mitigated by the existence of global markets, nevertheless, under plausible assumptions, a country's regulatory stringency is likely to have a disproportionate impact on its domestic firms. There seems to be a rough negative correlation between the stringency of a country's price controls and the innovative success of its domestic pharmaceutical industry. There is little dispute that the United States, which has had free pricing, has been the leader in drug innovation. Among the major countries of the European Union,

---

10. These direct sales figures exclude sales of French products marked under license to foreign companies. Since licensed products are omitted for all countries, the omission should not bias the comparison between countries.

France and Italy have had among the most stringent regulatory regimes and have performed relatively poorly in terms of true innovation, although France has produced a considerable number of minor products. Similarly, Japan has produced a large number of new drugs but few global drugs. The U.K. has excelled in innovation and development of global products. Although many factors may contribute to the innovative success of U.K. pharmaceutical firms, the structure of the U.K. rate-of-return regulation scheme, which was designed to encourage R&D, has plausibly been an important contributing factor.[11] Whether the positive influence of the PPRS on innovation will survive recent changes remains to be seen.

---

11. For a comparison of regulatory systems in France and the U.K., see Hancher (1990).

6
Effects of Regulation on Productivity

A secondary objective of regulatory systems in several countries, in addition to control of drug expenditures, is to promote industrial policy goals of domestic investment and employment. France and Italy, for example, grant higher prices for products that are produced locally, notwithstanding EEC stipulations against such bias. Similarly, the U.K.'s rate-of-return regulation favors firms that locate their capital in that country. Theory and evidence from other industries suggest that such input-based regulation tends to distort managerial decisions away from cost-minimizing input choices, where such distortions are rewarded by higher prices. The net effect is to increase costs and to reduce productivity.

Anecdotal evidence and previous analysis are consistent with these predictions. Burstall and Reuben (1988) conclude that multinational pharmaceutical companies operate many plants in Europe at one-third to one-half of capacity, partly because of government pressure to maintain local production. Consolidation of underutilized manufacturing facilities is a major cost-cutting objective of pharmaceutical firms, in response to the global squeeze on revenues from tighter regulation in Europe and more aggressive managed care in the United States.

This chapter provides more detailed evidence on the effects of biased regulation on productivity and returns to capital. We compare France, Italy, and the U.K., examples of countries with biased regulation, with Germany and the

United States, benchmark countries where pricing is either free or constrained in ways that are neutral toward resource use and plant location. To distinguish effects of regulation from other factors that may contribute to cross-national productivity differences, we compare pharmaceuticals to other manufacturing that is not subject to the same regulatory constraints.

The evidence strongly suggests that regulation has distorted resource use and hence has significantly reduced productivity in pharmaceuticals relative to other industries, particularly in France. Of significant interest is that these excess costs appear to be borne, at least in part, in the form of lower returns to the sunk capital that is invested by multinational firms in global R&D.

Incentive Effects of Biased Regulation

Biased regulation that offers higher prices in return for domestic production creates incentives for the pharmaceutical firm to accept excessive input costs.[1] The incentive for a firm rationally to trade off excess production costs for higher prices can be illustrated with a simple model. Consider a firm that produces output Q with two variable inputs, labor L and capital K, and a technology-related fixed input M, subject to the production function $Q(L,K;M)$ and constant factor prices W_L and W_K. With biased regulation, output price $P(L,K;M)$ is increasing in domestic employment of L and K with $P_{Xi}>0, P_{Xi,Xi}\leq0$, $Xi=L,K$. For simplicity assume that Q is independent of P. The firm selects L and K to maximize profits R:

$$R = P(L,K;M)Q(L,K;M) - W_L - W_K \qquad (6\text{--}1)$$

In the absence of regulation, a firm's optimal employment of any factor, such as labor or capital, balances the value

---

1. This section summarizes results discussed in more detail in Danzon and Percy (1996).

of that factor's marginal product against its marginal cost or wage. Regulation acts by reducing the effective marginal cost of the favored input:

$$PdQ/dX_i = w_i - dP/dX_i Q \qquad (6\text{--}2)$$

where X_i denotes any outcome. Thus, with biased regulation the profit-maximizing firm expands employment beyond the usual equality between the value of the marginal product and the marginal factor cost. The excess is greater, the greater the price increase that is granted in return for job creation. The percentage increase in manufacturing costs that a firm would willingly incur, in return for a given percentage increase in price, is greater, the lower the manufacturing cost as a percentage of total costs. Thus, regulators have proportionately greater "taxing" power for innovative drugs, which incur relatively higher R&D costs than manufacturing costs. If manufacturing costs are 25 percent of total costs, for example, a firm would accept up to a 20 percent increase in manufacturing costs in return for a 5 percent increase in price.

The details of the regulations in different countries encourage different distortions. The U.K. rate-of-return regulation favors excessive local investments in manufacturing and R&D capital. Price regulation in France and Italy could lead to excessive local plant capacity as well as excessive job creation. The distorting effects of regulation are likely to be greatest for multinational firms because domestic firms would, in any case, voluntarily locate more of their operations in their home country. The distortions are also expected to be concentrated in secondary production (processing and packaging) rather than in primary production, which is subject to greater economies of scale and tax reasons for location in particular countries. To some extent, regulation may simply result in a relocation of production from a neutral country, say Germany, to a biased country, say France. Such substitution across countries implies less adverse effects on costs and productivity than if all countries demand local production, such that capacity is duplicated in different countries.

Data and Empirical Methods

The effects of regulation on productivity are examined here using OECD data on input levels and productivity (value added) for pharmaceuticals and total manufacturing for the period 1970–1990. The four European countries—France, Italy, the U.K., and West Germany—have similar populations and similar opportunities for export within the EU. Although the U.S. market is much larger than the domestic market of any single European country, the total EU market represents larger total sales volume than the United States. Thus, opportunities for economies of scale should be similar, in the absence of regulatory distortions toward domestic production and barriers to exports. For this analysis, the subsidiaries of multinational firms are allocated to the country in which they operate since this placement corresponds to the scope of the regulation.

Although OECD data on outputs and inputs are the best available, they are not ideal for the purpose at hand. Value added is defined as gross output minus the cost of materials, energy, and supplies. Other inputs, such as contracted services, licensing, and royalty fees, are reflected in value added. Labor is measured as the number of employees, unadjusted for hours worked or skill mix.[2] We use the reported measure of gross fixed capital formation to estimate the stock of capital and assume that the flow of

---

2. For the United States, the OECD data exclude Puerto Rico, which accounted for roughly 14 percent of U.S. production and 9 percent of employment in pharmaceuticals in the 1980s. We report results adjusted to include Puerto Rico where data are available. Conclusions are not significantly affected.

capital services is proportional to the stock.[3] The most significant omission on the input side is the lack of a measure of value of the stock of R&D capital. These GDP measures of value added, by country of operation, focus on productivity in operations and do not attempt to measure productivity in developing innovative new drugs, as discussed in chapter 5.

Ideally, we want to measure the effects of regulation on productivity. In practice, the observed productivity differentials may also reflect factors other than regulation. These contaminating factors include cross-country differences in mix of primary and secondary production;[4] imperfect pharmaceutical-specific price indexes; differences in product mix and industry structure, which may themselves be influenced by regulation; and unmeasured R&D activities. If either productivity or regulation-induced inefficiencies differ between multinational and domestic firms, for example, then estimates of the impact of regulation may be affected by a country's product mix.

Empirical Results

Employment. Between 1980 and 1990, pharmaceutical employment grew almost three times more rapidly in France (15.8 percent) than in the United States (5.8 per-

---

3. The capital stock in year t is estimated as: $K_t = (1 - d)K_{t-1} + I_t$, and $K_0 = (1/d)I_{1-3}$, where I_{1-3} is the mean of gross investment in the first three years. The estimates of the depreciation rate (d) are based on the country-specific depreciation rates for equipment and structures reported in Berndt and Hesse (1986). We assume a weight 0.67 for equipment and 0.33 for structures. We also estimate results based on a uniform ten-year life of capital.

4. Reported value added is relatively high for primary production because the input costs of bulk chemicals are low, whereas the output is valued to reflect the intangible value of the embodied R&D. Location of primary production plants is generally dictated by tax considerations. The data do not permit us to distinguish between primary and secondary production.

TABLE 6–1
GROWTH IN NUMBER OF EMPLOYEES IN SELECTED COUNTRIES,
1975–1990
(1980 = 100)

Country	1975	1980	1985	1990
France				
Total manufacturing	106.2	100.0	88.1	83.5
Drugs and medicines[a]	101.9[b]	100.0	106.8	115.8
Germany				
Total manufacturing	100.0	100.0	92.9	98.3
Drugs and medicines	105.1[b]	100.0	104.5	113.4
Italy				
Total manufacturing	94.7	100.0	85.0	85.2
Drugs and medicines[a]	101.4[b]	100.0	97.0	104.2[b]
United Kingdom				
Total manufacturing	108.1	100.0	78.5	77.6
Drugs and medicines[a]	90.0	100.0	91.4	103.5
United States				
Total manufacturing	89.5	100.0	94.7	95.0
Drugs and medicines[a]	86.7	100.0	94.8	105.8

a. Survey based data; may not be national accounts compatible.
b. Figures are estimated using the ratio of drugs and medicines to other chemicals for the closest year for which data are available.
SOURCE: OECD STAN database. See Danzon and Percy (1996).

cent) and the U.K. (3.5 percent) (table 6–1). By 1990, the share of pharmaceutical employment in total manufacturing employment was 2.0 percent in France, 1.38 percent in the U.K., and 1.3 percent in Italy, compared with only 1.15 percent in Germany and 0.95 percent in the United States (excluding Puerto Rico). Although this employment growth in pharmaceuticals may appear to vindicate France's use of regulation for industrial policy purposes, these data do not reveal how much is a net gain, rather than simply a diversion from other sectors.

Value Added. In all countries, total value added in pharmaceuticals grew relative to other manufacturing industries over this period. The precise measure of growth in real value added is sensitive to the price index used to convert current local currency units to constant value. The GDP deflator represents economywide inflation in each country. Where pharmaceutical price inflation either leads or lags general inflation, however, using this GDP deflator leads to upward or downward biased estimates of real productivity growth in pharmaceuticals. We therefore report some results using a drugs-specific producer price index (PPI).

A measure that is independent of the price index is the cumulative increase in value added relative to the cumulative increase in the total value of production. For the 1980s, this ratio was 0.58 in Italy, 0.87 in France, 1.06 in the United States, 1.12 in the U.K., and 1.13 in Germany. Thus, in France and Italy, value added declined over this period, as a share of total value of production, while it grew in other countries.

Value Added per Employee. Table 6–2 compares labor productivity levels relative to the United States, converting at purchasing power parities (PPPs). Value added per employee in pharmaceuticals is more than twice as high in the United States as in all European countries. Of the European countries, the U.K. leads with value added per employee at 47 percent of the United States, followed by Germany at 33.2 percent, Italy at 28.7 percent, and France at 19.8 percent.[5] This shortfall of labor productivity in Europe relative to the United States is much greater in pharmaceuticals than in other manufacturing sectors. For total manufacturing, the 1990 figures for European productivity relative to the United States are 92.7 percent for

---

5. Adding Puerto Rico raises U.S. value added by about three percentage points (1987 data), as expected, given the tax incentives to locate high value-added operations in Puerto Rico.

TABLE 6–2
VALUE ADDED PER EMPLOYEE IN SELECTED COUNTRIES, RELATIVE TO
THE UNITED STATES, 1970–1990
(UNITED STATES = 100)

Country	1970	1975	1980	1985	1990
France					
Total manufacturing	70.5	71.7	79.4	79.9	92.7
Drugs and medicines[a]	—	23.2[b]	29.8	21.7	19.8
Germany					
Total manufacturing	63.9	66.3	73.3	74.3	77.2
Drugs and medicines	—	36.8[b]	42.7	36.2	33.2
Italy					
Total manufacturing	60.8	64.0	76.6	76.3	79.4
Drugs and medicines[b,c]	—	39.9[b]	43.7	38.4	28.7[b]
United Kingdom					
Total manufacturing	47.1	48.6	51.6	57.5	62.6
Drugs and medicines[b,c]	37.0	41.3	49.1	47.4	47.0

NOTE: PPP currency conversion.
a. Survey-based employment data; may not be national accounts compatible.
b. Figures estimated using the ratio of drugs and medicines to other chemicals for the closest year for which data are available.
c. Survey-based value-added data; may not be national accounts compatible.
SOURCE: Author's calculations using OECD STAN data. See Danzon and Percy (1996).

France, 79.4 percent for Italy, 77.2 percent for Germany, and 62.6 percent for the U.K.

Since value added is measured at local prices, the lower prices for pharmaceuticals in France, Italy, and the United Kingdom contribute to these countries' low measures of value added per employee, relative to the United States. To control for this, table 6–3 shows value added per employee, relative to the United States, adjusted to U.S. price levels using Fisher indexes. Although this adjustment dramatically improves the European productivity measures, Germany is still only 60 percent of the

TABLE 6–3
VALUE ADDED PER EMPLOYEE IN SELECTED COUNTRIES,
RELATIVE TO THE UNITED STATES, 1981–1990
(UNITED STATES = 100)

Country	1981	1985[a]	1990
France[b]	50.7	38.0	64.2
Germany	39.2	34.0	59.6
Italy[b,c]	61.2	54.4	72.5[d]
United Kingdom[b,c]	52.3	56.2	83.6
United States[b,c]	100.0	100.0	100.0

NOTE: Currency conversion with Fisher price indexes for pharmaceuticals.

a. 1985 Fisher indexes were estimated by taking average of 1984 and 1986.

b. Survey-based employment data; may not be national accounts compatible.

c. Survey-based value-added data; may not be national accounts compatible.

d. Figures estimated using the ratio of drugs and medicines to other chemicals for the closest year for which data are available.

Local currencies converted to U.S. dollars using GDP PPPs in table 6–2, current exchange rates, and Fisher indexes of relative pharmaceutical prices in table 6–3.

SOURCE: OECD STAN database. See Danzon and Percy (1996).

United States, 64 percent for France, 73 percent for Italy, and 84 percent for the U.K. These figures for productivity in pharmaceuticals are still generally lower than for total manufacturing.[6] Moreover, while adjusting to comparable price levels is appropriate for cross-national comparisons, productivity valued at local prices as in table 6–2 is the correct measure for evaluating relative productivity across industries and efficiency of resource allocation within a country.

---

6. Table 6–3 may understate the productivity shortfall in price-regulated economies such as France and Italy because the pharmaceutical price indexes used, based only on matching products, may understate relative prices if global products are more stringently regulated than domestic products.

TABLE 6–4
GROWTH IN GROSS FIXED CAPITAL FORMATION IN SELECTED
COUNTRIES, 1975–1990
(1980 = 100)

Country	1975	1980	1985	1990
France				
Total manufacturing	83.3	100.0	94.4	132.6
Drugs and medicines[a]	—	100.0	156.7	250.1
Germany				
Total manufacturing	76.2	100.0	96.4	132.6
Drugs and medicines	—	100.0	119.5	136.2
United Kingdom				
Total manufacturing	95.9	100.0	100.8	108.3
Drugs and medicines[a]	76.2	100.0	131.5	161.9
United States				
Total manufacturing	75.3	100.0	93.4	101.7
Drugs and medicines[a]	76.8	100.0	123.9	160.4

NOTES: Gross fixed capital formation is national accounts compatible (land, buildings, machinery, and equipment). Real GDP-deflator-adjusted values.
a. Capital formation figures are survey-based data; may not be national accounts compatible.
SOURCE: Author's calculations using OECD STAN data. See Danzon and Percy (1996).

Capital Formation. Between 1980 and 1990, fixed capital formation in pharmaceuticals increased 150 percent in France,[7] compared with 60 percent in the United States and 62 percent in the U.K. (table 6–4). In France, capital formation has grown more rapidly in pharmaceuticals (150 percent) than in total manufacturing (33 percent) and has even outpaced the rapid growth in pharmaceutical employment. Consequently, capital per employee (table 6–5) in France increased 116 percent in pharma-

---

7. The 1990 figure of 250 for France is above trend; the three-year average for 1989–1991 is 237. Using this lower figure would not affect the conclusions.

TABLE 6–5
GROWTH IN GROSS FIXED CAPITAL FORMATION PER EMPLOYEE IN
SELECTED COUNTRIES, 1975–1990
(1980 = 100)

Country	1975	1980	1985	1990
France				
Total manufacturing	78.5	100.0	107.2	158.8
Drugs and medicines[a,b]	—	100.0	146.8	215.9
Germany				
Total manufacturing	76.1	100.0	103.8	134.9
Drugs and medicines	—	100.0	114.3	120.1
United Kingdom				
Total manufacturing	88.8	100.0	128.3	139.7
Drugs and medicines[a,b]	84.4	100.0	143.9	156.3
United States				
Total manufacturing	84.1	100.0	98.7	107.1
Drugs and medicines[a,b]	88.6	100.0	130.7	151.7

NOTES: Gross fixed capital formation is national accounts compatible
(land, buildings, machinery, and equipment). Real GDP-deflator–
adjusted values.
a. Capital formation figures are survey-based data; may not be national
accounts compatible.
b. Employment figures are survey-based data; may not be national accounts compatible.
SOURCE: OECD STAN database. See Danzon and Percy (1996).

ceuticals, compared with 20 percent in Germany, 56 percent in the U.K., and 52 percent in the U.S. Nevertheless,
over the same decade, French value added per employee
has increased less in pharmaceuticals than in manufacturing. The slow growth in labor productivity in pharmaceuticals in France relative to Germany and the U.K. (table
6–3) has occurred despite a more rapid increase in capital
per employee in France.

Between 1980 and 1990, the U.K. also experienced
more rapid growth in capital formation in pharmaceuticals (62 percent) than in total manufacturing (8 percent).
Pharmaceuticals also experienced more rapid growth in

capital formation per employee than did other manufacturing in the U.K. This pattern is consistent with the predicted effects of rate-of-return regulation. This growth in capital per employee probably contributed to the U.K. pharmaceutical industry's rapid growth in labor productivity.

For Germany, growth in capital formation between 1980 and 1990 has been similar in pharmaceuticals (35 percent) and total manufacturing (33 percent), although capital formation per employee grew less in pharmaceuticals than in other manufacturing (20 percent compared with 35 percent). Nevertheless, value added per employee has grown more in pharmaceuticals than in other manufacturing (33 percent compared with 18 percent) in Germany. Moreover, despite lower growth in capital per employee in Germany than in France, Germany's growth in labor productivity in pharmaceuticals relative to the United States outpaced that of France.

Although the low labor productivity growth in pharmaceuticals in France relative to Germany certainly cannot be explained by slower growth in capital per employee, the low labor productivity in the French and German pharmaceutical sectors, relative to the United States, may be influenced by lower capital-labor ratios in these countries. Relative to the United States, capital formation per employee in pharmaceuticals is 57 percent for France, 49 percent for Germany, and 99 percent for the U.K. By contrast, for total manufacturing, capital formation per employee relative to the United States is 125 percent in France, 84 percent in Germany, and only 65 percent in the U.K. For Germany, whereas capital formation per employee in total manufacturing has increased relative to the United States (from 61 percent in 1975 to 84 percent in 1990), for pharmaceuticals the trend is reversed, dropping from 79 percent of the U.S. level in 1975 to 40 percent in 1988 and 49 percent in 1989. This evidence is consistent with the hypothesis that pharmaceuti-

TABLE 6–6
LABOR COMPENSATION PER EMPLOYEE IN SELECTED COUNTRIES,
RELATIVE TO THE UNITED STATES, 1970–1990
(UNITED STATES = 100)

Country	1970	1975	1980	1985	1990
France					
Total manufacturing	57.3	66.5	73.3	75.3	84.4
Drugs and medicines[a]	—	76.5	89.0	84.5	86.1
Germany					
Total manufacturing	53.7	60.8	68.4	70.4	77.1
Drugs and medicines	—	71.0	67.6	64.2	65.4
Italy					
Total manufacturing	47.4	59.5	58.9	60.1	65.5
Drugs and medicines[a]	—	—	—	—	—
United Kingdom					
Total manufacturing	49.6	57.6	55.6	60.1	67.9
Drugs and medicines[a]	41.1	56.7	61.3	68.8	78.0

NOTES: Labor compensation is national accounts compatible labor
costs. PPP currency conversion.
a. Employment figures are survey-based data; may not be national accounts compatible.
SOURCE: OECD database. See Danzon and Percy (1996).

cal investments have been diverted from Germany to
other EU countries with biased regulation. Other unmeasured factors may also contribute.

R&D investments per employee are roughly twice as
high in the United States as in the other countries. This is
consistent with the evidence (see below) that returns to
R&D investments are higher in the United States than in
these European countries.

Labor Compensation. Comparing labor compensation
and productivity in other countries relative to the United
States (table 6–6), in France there is little difference in
labor compensation between pharmaceuticals (86 percent) and total manufacturing (84 percent), despite

much lower value added per employee in pharmaceuticals (20–64 percent) than for French manufacturing in general (93 percent). In Germany, labor compensation relative to the United States in 1990 is lower in pharmaceuticals (65 percent) than in total manufacturing (77 percent). In the U.K., labor compensation relative to the United States is 78 percent in pharmaceuticals, compared with 68 percent in total manufacturing, but this roughly matches productivity differences. Thus, French employees in pharmaceuticals appear to be paid more, relative to their productivity, than French employees in other industries and more than pharmaceutical employees in other countries.

Returns to Capital. Measuring the return to capital in pharmaceuticals is problematic because a significant fraction of pharmaceutical capital is intangible capital, including investments in R&D, promotion, and reputation. The difference between the reported measures of value added and labor compensation reflects returns to both this unmeasured, intangible capital and returns to tangible physical capital. Although data on the flow of R&D expenditures are available, these data do not yield an accurate measure of the stock of R&D capital available in each country because of lags between R&D investments and production of marketable products and, more important, because the value of each country's R&D investments is disseminated to other countries through global products that are sold directly or under license. Thus, the stock of R&D knowledge available in France, for example, reflects not only prior R&D investments in France but also prior R&D in the United States, the United Kingdom, Switzerland, and other countries, embodied in patents that are used for producing global products in France.

To illustrate the problem of omitted intangible capital, table 6–7 shows the implied, hypothetical rate of return to measured, physical capital estimated under the

TABLE 6–7
HYPOTHETICAL EX POST RETURN TO PHYSICAL CAPITAL, ASSUMING
NO INTANGIBLE CAPITAL, 1976–1990
(percent)

Country	1976–80	1981–85	1986–90
France			
Total manufacturing	27	23	29
Drugs and medicines			
GDP deflator	10	7	7
PPI drugs	n.a.	19	36
Germany			
Total manufacturing	34	29	31
Drugs and medicines			
GDP deflator	52	59	71
PPI drugs	n.a.	59	74
Italy			
Total manufacturing	22	23	27
Drugs and medicines			
GDP deflator	n.a.	n.a.	n.a.
PPI drugs	n.a.	n.a.	n.a.
United Kingdom			
Total manufacturing	18	17	23
Drugs and medicines			
GDP deflator	66	63	73
PPI drugs	n.a.	68	97
United States			
Total manufacturing	27	24	29
Drugs and medicines			
GDP deflator	128	138	169
PPI drugs	n.a.	128	121

NOTE: Return to capital = (value added – labor compensation)/capital stock. Depreciation rate = 10%.
SOURCE: Danzon and Percy (1996).

assumption that there is no intangible capital, such that the full difference between value added and labor compensation accrues to physical capital. For pharmaceuticals, estimates are reported based on both the GDP deflator and the producer price index for pharmaceuticals. Using the GDP deflator, this estimated return to physical capital in France is much lower for pharmaceuticals (7 percent) than for total manufacturing (29 percent), whereas the reverse is true in other countries, particularly the United States, where the implied return to capital invested in pharmaceuticals is implausibly large.[8] The same conclusions hold with the PPI-based estimates, although the differences across countries are less extreme. This evidence in table 6–7 is not intended to—and does not—provide credible estimates of the return to capital in different countries because measured capital includes only physical capital in plant, equipment, and land. The implausibly large estimates do confirm, however, that intangible capital such as R&D is an important omitted input in pharmaceuticals. Returns to this input in France are below levels in other countries and below levels in other manufacturing industries in France, plausibly because of price regulation.

Conclusions

The evidence supports the hypothesis that biased price regulation has led to excessive use of capital and labor in France and that this has reduced productivity. Capital and employment in France have grown rapidly in pharmaceuticals relative to other manufacturing despite much lower productivity per worker in pharmaceuticals. Capital-labor ratios in pharmaceuticals have grown more in France than in Germany, the U.K., and the United States (data for Italy are not available). By 1990, capital-labor ratios were higher in France than in Germany for pharmaceuticals, but labor productivity was 13 percentage points lower in

---

8. These general conclusions are robust whether capital stock is estimated using constant ten- or fifteen-year life of capital or country-specific lives based on depreciation rates from Berndt and Hesse (1986).

France if measured at purchasing power parity (PPP) values.

For the United Kingdom, regulation appears to have affected input levels, as predicted, but without adverse effects on productivity. Although capital investment has been rapid in the United Kingdom, growth in total factor productivity in pharmaceuticals has been at least as high as in the United States and higher than in other manufacturing in the United Kingdom. Value added per employee, relative to the United States, is higher for pharmaceuticals than for other manufacturing in the United Kingdom. One plausible explanation is that rate-of-return regulation in the United Kingdom has encouraged highly productive forms of capital investment, whereas the price regulatory system in France has merely encouraged excess secondary production capacity and job creation. Relative to the United States, the United Kingdom has higher value added per employee for pharmaceuticals than does any other country studied here, whereas this is not true for other manufacturing in the U.K.

Low pharmaceutical prices in France certainly contribute to the low value added. For cross-country comparisons of productivity levels, the gap between labor productivity in pharmaceuticals in France and Germany is eliminated if local currencies are converted using a drug-specific price index rather than the PPPs. While this adjustment may be relevant for evaluating real productivity, however, it is not relevant for evaluating the distortions in resource allocation between industries within a single country.

The low rates of labor productivity in pharmaceuticals relative to other sectors in France are not matched by low compensation. Compensation per worker (relative to the United States) is comparable in pharmaceuticals and in total manufacturing, although French value added per

81

worker is much higher in manufacturing than in pharmaceuticals.

What accounts for the low productivity in the French pharmaceutical industry relative to other manufacturing in France or pharmaceuticals in other countries? One possible contributing factor is the relatively large market share of domestic products in France. The production technology for these domestic products could entail lower productivity, which, in turn, reduces overall average pharmaceutical productivity in France.[9] Whether regulation contributes to this large market share of domestic products, which are plausibly of lower therapeutic merit, is an interesting question for future research. The other possible contributing factor is the distortion engendered by regulatory pressures placed on multinational companies: too many plants, excess capacity, and inefficient production techniques. These distortions lead to low productivity even for global products, which could potentially have higher productivity. These two factors are not mutually exclusive, and, in practice, both probably contribute to the low observed productivity in French pharmaceuticals.

A second question emerges from these data: How can market forces support the net inflow of labor in France during the 1980s into the pharmaceutical sector, which is relatively unproductive, from other manufacturing sectors where labor is more productive, both absolutely and relative to the compensation received? Here, again, regulation appears to play a role. If labor is paid more, relative to its marginal product, in pharmaceuticals than in other sectors of French industry and this differential does not exist in pharmaceutical sectors in other countries, then other factors must receive less in the pharmaceutical sec-

---

9. Some of these local products may be similar to products classified in the United States as vitamins, nutrients, and hematinic preparations (SIC 2837). These have relatively low productivity: they account for 20 percent of employees and 20 percent of new capital expenditures but only 9 percent of value added in SIC 283 (1987 data).

tor in France. Supplies and variable capital inputs must earn a normal return. Thus, the residual factor is the sunk investment in R&D for products that are currently on the market. In the long run, however, domestic firms that produce products solely for the French market will incur only those R&D costs that are commensurate with the low rate of return for R&D investments. Thus, only relatively non-innovative products will be developed for the French market, consistent with the theory and empirical evidence in chapter 5. For global products that are sold in other major markets, returns on the sunk R&D investments in global products can be driven to zero in France, as long as revenues in other markets of the world are sufficient to yield a normal overall return on the R&D investments.

These data suggest that regulation in France has not only yielded low prices for consumers but has also contributed to excessive employment of labor and physical capital in the French pharmaceutical sector. The resulting excess costs have been borne by the suppliers of capital who invested in the R&D that produced global products. The issue here goes beyond the question of the contribution by various countries to paying for the common costs of R&D from which they all benefit. A country may pay prices only sufficient to compensate the variable inputs for the value of their marginal product, assuming efficient production. In the case of France, regulation appears to have resulted not only in low prices but also in excessive employment, leading to productivity that would not support the level of compensation were it not for the availability of other common, fixed factors financed outside the country. This strategy clearly cannot be pursued in major markets for an indefinite period without adverse effects on innovative R&D.

7
Cross-national Multiplier Effects of Regulation

B ecause of the global nature of innovative drugs, the regulation of pharmaceutical prices in one country directly affects the revenues of research-based pharmaceutical firms regardless of their country of origin. In addition to this direct effect, indirect effects occur when low prices in one country spill over to affect prices in other countries. These spillovers are growing as governments in countries that have had traditionally relatively high drug prices increasingly employ policies that use low foreign prices to hold down their own drug prices. These spillovers imply a multiplier effect: stringent regulation in one country can reduce the total global revenues of multinational drug firms by a factor that is many times larger than the direct effect in the country that initiates the regulation.

Two policies are used to achieve these regulatory spillovers. The first uses international price comparisons as a benchmark for regulating prices in the domestic market. Canada and Italy already apply such schemes, and the same approach has been proposed for Japan. In the United States, President Clinton's Health Security Act (HSA, 1993) proposed an Advisory Council on Breakthrough New Drugs, which would determine whether U.S. prices are reasonable using several criteria, including prices in more than twenty foreign countries.

The second strategy permits parallel importing of drugs from lower-price countries, such as France or

Greece, into higher-price countries, such as the U.K., Germany, and the Netherlands. Parallel trade has been upheld by the European Court of Justice as consistent with principles of free trade. Actual parallel trade flows were only 5 percent of total EEC sales in 1992 (SNIP 1993) but may exceed 20 percent in traditionally higher-price markets such as the U.K. The potential impact of parallel trade has increased significantly with the launch of the European Medicines Agency in 1995, which can grant simultaneous approval of new drugs throughout the EU, and with the accession to the EU of low-price countries, such as Spain and, potentially, countries of Eastern Europe. Parallel trade may become an issue in other trading blocks, such as the North American Free Trade Area.

This chapter examines the economic effects of these policies that have the effect of equalizing drug prices across countries. Contrary to standard free trade arguments, permitting parallel trade is unlikely to enhance economic well-being when the price differentials largely reflect regulatory differences. Similarly, regulation based on international price comparisons undermines the price differentials that are required for the optimal recoupment of the joint costs of R&D (see chapter 2). Since such regulatory policies are likely to continue, however, options to mitigate their adverse effects are considered.

Welfare Implications of Parallel Trade

Price and Quality Effects. In general, trade increases economic well-being, assuming that (a) consumers in the importing country benefit from the lower prices or greater range of products in the exporting country and (b) these lower prices reflect either greater production efficiency or lower input costs in the exporting country.

These conditions for trade to be welfare-enhancing are commonly violated in the case of parallel trade in drugs. First, the lower foreign prices largely reflect regulatory stringency, not superior production efficiency—indeed, strict price regulation tends to reduce production efficiency, as demonstrated in chapter 6. In fact, because parallel trade entails intermediation costs to arbitrage price differences that do not reflect real cost savings, it can actually increase total social costs but still be profitable for the trader. "Parallel trade has become so great that eight in ten High Street chemists in Britain regularly dispense drugs made in Britain, exported to France, say, and re-imported for sale to NHS patients (in Britain)" (Pallot 1992). Second, the savings from lower prices often accrue largely to intermediaries—parallel traders, wholesalers, and retail pharmacists—and not to consumers or payers in the importing country, who continue to pay the (higher) regulated price, at least in the short run. International price comparisons might appear to benefit consumers in the high-price country if the prices they pay are directly regulated based on the lower foreign prices. This, however, ignores long-run effects.

In the long run, a manufacturer's best strategy when faced with the threat of parallel trade or international price comparisons is to attempt to set a uniform price in all countries that are linked by either trade or price comparisons in order to minimize the revenue loss from the regulatory spillovers that would occur if differential pricing were attempted. The potential revenue loss is greater, the more heterogeneous are the markets that are linked, and particularly if the major markets of Europe, the United States, and Japan are affected.

To illustrate, assume that international price comparisons are the basis for price regulation in both the United States and Japan, which together account for roughly 60 percent of sales of global products. If prices in France are, say, 40 percent lower than in these countries and France accounts for 5 percent of sales of global drugs, then the French pricing policy would reduce global revenues by 26 percent ($.65 \times .4$), not 2 percent ($.05 \times .4$), which is the direct effect from the French market alone.

Theory suggests that if a manufacturer is constrained by parallel trade or international price comparisons to charge a single price for a drug, that price will lie between the prices that would have been charged in the separate markets in the absence of the constraint. It might, thus, appear that consumers in the initially higher-price country ultimately do benefit from lower prices because of parallel trade or international price comparisons. But, in the long run, these consumers are worse off if these lower prices result in lower investments in R&D and hence less availability of new drugs that they would have been willing to pay for.

Consumers in the traditionally low-price country are also worse off because they are now faced with a higher price. If governments in these countries are unwilling to pay the higher price, the launch of new products is likely to be delayed or even totally abandoned in these countries, leading to loss of access for consumers to the innovative drugs, although they may be willing to pay a price that covers their marginal cost. Companies may rationally choose to abandon small markets that contribute minimally to global revenues rather than accept prices that would pull down the revenues that can be achieved in other, larger markets.

These predictions are borne out by recent empirical evidence that several major manufacturers are pursuing uniform price policies for new drugs. In France, for example, Glaxo's refusal to accept a relatively low price for its new migraine drug Imigran has delayed launch for several years despite marketing approval. This delay results in forgone health benefits to French consumers and forgone revenues to the manufacturer that can never be recouped because the patent clock keeps ticking despite delays in launch.

In addition to price effects, parallel trade may reduce information, services, and ultimately the quality of care for consumers. Parallel trade makes it easier for counterfeit manufacturers to enter the supply chain because regulators do not require chemical testing for equivalence of parallel imports. In addition, parallel trade undermines the incentives of drug distributors in each country—licensees or subsidiaries of multinationals—to invest in providing information and support to medical practitioners. If the drugs for the German market can be imported from France, for example, the German subsidiary receives no return on investments in providing information to physicians, maintaining the company's reputation for service and reliability, etc. The need to stabilize demand among different distributors of a manufacturer's products, in order to create appropriate incentives for each distributor to invest in customer service and quality, is widely recognized in the literature on exclusive dealerships.[1] It is another reason why manufacturers are likely to move to a uniform pricing policy when faced with the threat of parallel trade.

Price Differences Do Not Imply Cost Shifting. It is often argued that price differences between countries or between users within a country reflect cost shifting: "A pharmaceutical company may only be willing to sell in a low price country because it can recoup any losses it makes there from sales in higher priced countries" (Brittan 1992). This argument either ignores the problem of joint costs or mistakenly assumes that they should be allocated equally to all users.

From the long-run perspective of the firm trying to estimate whether prices on average will be sufficient to justify the costs of developing a new drug, if low-price countries cover at least their marginal costs and make some contribution to the joint costs, prices in high-price countries can actually be *lower* than they would have to be

---

1. See also Rozek and Rapp (1992).

to cover joint costs in the absence of contributions from the low-price market. Thus, from the predevelopment perspective, the cost-shifting argument is backward.

Similarly, the cost-shifting argument is also mistaken when applied to the issue of pricing a product already on the market. Consider the problem for a profit-maximizing firm that can set different prices in two separate markets. The profit-maximizing price in each market depends only on its own price elasticity and is lower in the more price-sensitive (elastic) market than in the less price-sensitive (inelastic) market. To attempt to raise the price in the inelastic market to "recoup losses" from the lower price in the other market would actually *reduce* net revenues, compared to pricing for each market separately, based solely on its own price elasticity.[2] Thus, viewing pricing from either a long-run perspective (deciding which products to develop) or a short-run perspective (pricing existing products), the cost-shifting argument assumes behavior that is inconsistent with profit-maximization by firms.[3]

Policy Options

Parallel Trade. The first best policy option would be to exempt pharmaceuticals from parallel trade. A similar exemption should apply to other industries that exhibit the same characteristics—the importance of R&D and intellectual property, combined with regulated prices. If parallel trade continues to be permitted, however, then it is worth considering policy options that would reduce the welfare losses to consumers that are likely if manufacturers adopt a uniform price policy to deter parallel trade.

One possible strategy is for manufacturers to pay re-

2. For a similar argument applied to health care more generally, see Morrisey (1994).

3. For a similar application of this argument applied to the allegation of cost shifting by hospitals, see Phelps (1986) and Dranove (1988). For a discussion of price differentials in drugs more generally, see Berndt (1994) and Danzon (1995).

bates directly to governments (or their surrogates) in countries where lower prices are appropriate, while maintaining a uniform list price. This practice targets the discounts directly at purchasers who are intended to benefit, while eliminating arbitrage opportunities for traders. Similar methods are widely used in other industries to achieve price differentials. Many consumer products, for example, are sold with a coupon that must be submitted to the manufacturer for a rebate. Since only the price-sensitive buyers take the time to send in the coupon, this practice achieves ex post price differentials based on price sensitivity. Similarly, discounts from list prices are given price-sensitive drug benefit managers in the United States, with the rebates paid directly to the purchaser-payer—usually an insurer, managed-care company, or employer. Although such rebate systems have been attacked in anti–discount-pricing bills, these bills ignore the potential welfare gains from price differentials in general and, in particular, as a mechanism for recouping joint costs.[4] A European precedent for such a scheme exists in the rebates provided to the former East Germany. These rebates lowered effective prices in the cast without encouraging parallel trade to the west. By permitting some price differentiation across countries, rebates would permit price-sensitive buyers to obtain lower prices and hence greater access to new drugs.

International Price Comparisons. If international price comparisons are to be performed and used by governments, then the criterion should be to permit differences that are plausibly consistent with optimal contributions to

---

4. The main proponents of anti–discount-pricing bills are retail pharmacists who mistakenly blame the loss in market share of small retail outlets on managed-care discounting. For an economic analysis of discount pricing for pharmaceuticals, see Berndt (1994) and Danzon (1995).

joint costs. This criterion does not yield precise guidelines. But it does suggest that comparisons should be limited to countries that are similar in characteristics that affect willingness to pay for innovative medical care, such as per capita income, medical norms, technologies, and spending levels. Comparisons should also take into account pricing patterns over the entire life-cycle of a drug. Real prices decline sharply over a drug's life-cycle in Japan, for example, whereas Canada permits inflation adjustments. To yield the same lifetime revenue, launch prices would have to be higher in Japan than in Canada. Moreover, if comparisons are used for regulatory purposes, they should be based on the full portfolio of a manufacturer's products, including all dosage forms and strengths, not on individual packs of specific drugs, which may be unrepresentative. Many costs are joint costs over a portfolio of drugs; hence, Ramsey pricing would permit these costs to be allocated differently in different countries, depending on their demand elasticities in the countries under comparison.

Finally, if comparisons are to be used for regulatory purposes, they should be based on exchange rates, not purchasing power parities. Exchange rates determine the innovator's actual revenues from foreign sales in terms of domestic currency and hence the contribution of different countries to joint costs of R&D. To ensure price stability to consumers and manufacturers, an average of monthly forward exchange rates for the relevant period can be used. By contrast, if prices were regulated based on PPPs and exchange rates deviated from PPPs, target contributions to joint costs would not be achieved. Moreover, opportunities for parallel trade would open up whenever the exchange rate fell significantly below the PPP, thus undermining the ability of manufacturers to pursue a uniform pricing policy. Similarly, prices that are set in European currency units would induce parallel trade whenever local currencies fluctuate significantly relative to the ECU.

8
Conclusions

The Uruguay Round of the negotiations on the General Agreement on Tariffs and Trade (GATT) reinforced and expanded protections for intellectual property, including patentable products of the research-based pharmaceutical industry. But these gains for the drug industry may be more than offset by the increasingly stringent regulation of drug prices and expenditures that governments in many countries are adopting. In their role as public insurers, governments may appropriately set some limits on how much they are willing to pay and for which drugs, in order to control insurance-induced overuse. Such policies, however, should be designed to balance the desire to control costs with the health concerns of individual patients today and the need to preserve incentives for innovation to develop the drugs for tomorrow. The forms of regulation adopted so far are not well designed to achieve these goals.

The pharmaceutical industry's high ratio of globally joint, sunk costs—mostly R&D—to user-specific marginal costs creates the opportunity and leverage for regulators and other major purchasers to force prices down to marginal costs. Prices can be forced below full cost in the short run without adversely affecting the supply of existing drugs or even the continued development of drugs already in the pipeline, which have already incurred a significant fraction of their R&D costs. Marginal cost pricing, however, would cover only 30 percent or less of total costs. In the long run, the supply of innovative new drugs will be adversely affected, although the full effects may not be evident for over a decade. Thus, whereas price controls in gasoline produce shortages that are local and immediately visible, the effects of drug price controls in one country on the supply of innovative drugs are diffuse and delayed and, hence, can easily be ignored. The supply of innovative drugs depends on global revenues and, in any case, responds with a lag of several years. This lack of immediate impact of low, local prices on supply creates strong temptations for regulators to focus on their own short-run budget savings, ignoring spillover effects to other countries and long-run effects on the global supply of innovations.

Small countries have and can pursue such free-rider strategies indefinitely without significantly affecting the long-run supply of innovative new drugs. But if the major markets of Europe, the United States, and Japan pursue similar strategies, then the global revenues of the industry will be severely undermined, and innovative R&D will likely be adversely affected. Of great immediate concern is that the aggressive regulatory strategies of some countries will spill over indirectly to other, traditionally higher-price markets, even without direct regulatory intervention in those countries, through parallel trade and international price comparisons. Parallel trade is often upheld on standard international trade grounds. This acceptance, however, ignores the fact that lower prices in some countries reflect more aggressive regulation, not greater efficiency in production. Moreover, such an attitude ignores the fact that optimal pricing to cover the joint costs of R&D requires that prices differ between countries or consumer groups, based on their price elasticity of demand. Uniform prices are not optimal, contrary to the common presumption. If enforced in practice, uniform prices will lead to the loss of some innovative drugs that consumers would be willing to pay for.

The traditional systems of price regulation have failed in their primary goal of controlling drug spending, which has risen more rapidly in France and Italy, which have regulated drug prices, than in Germany, the U.K., and the United States, which have permitted greater pricing freedom. Moreover, both countries with stringent price regulation have a dismal record of developing innovative drugs. Although France spends roughly the same percentage of sales on R&D as other countries, it has produced no innovative drugs in the past decade. Despite—or because of—rapid input growth, France has among the lowest productivity in operations of five major producing countries. This low productivity in France's pharmaceutical sector does not characterize its other manufacturing sectors.

It is too early to evaluate the full effects of the 1990s controls on drug expenditures that were adopted in Germany, the U.K., and France. Theory and preliminary evidence indicate that the strategy of defining global drug budgets and placing physicians at risk for overruns are successful at controlling drug spending. The cuts, however, are likely to fall disproportionately on innovative drugs, with implied adverse effects on patient care and on incentives for innovation.

The major policy challenge is to devise health insurance plans that control inappropriate use of drugs, while preserving appropriate access. Appropriate access includes availability—both present and future—of drugs that yield positive net social benefits, either because they reduce other medical costs, for example, by eliminating the need for costly hospitalization or because they yield benefits that patients are willing to pay for, either individually or collectively through social insurance plans.

The general trend in many European health care systems toward component budgeting—separate spending targets for drugs, hospital services, physician services, etc.—runs directly counter to the direction required to achieve efficient incentives for drug use and innovation. With separate global budgets or revenue limits for drugs, as in Germany and France, and indicative drug budgets for GPs in the U.K., physicians have incentives to reduce the drug budget regardless of whether this increases costs elsewhere in the medical system or other nonmedical costs for patients. Such component budgeting runs directly counter to an efficient incentive structure, which is to use the mix of medical services that best treats the patient's condition given the total target spending on health. Thus, if total medical costs can be reduced by spending more on drugs and less on inpatient care, this is the efficient direction to take. But, under component budgeting, each provider faces incentives to minimize the costs of the services for which they are responsible, without regard to—and, indeed, with incentives to shift costs to—other medical sectors.

In contrast to this move toward component budgeting in Europe, trends in the United States are more promising. The U.S. health care system is undergoing major restructuring, with the dominant trend being a move toward integrated delivery systems that are fully capitated and bear financial risk for the full continuum of care (Danzon, Greenberg, and Greenberg 1995). Such systems, in principle, face financial incentives to adopt the most efficient mix of services or, equivalently, to allocate their total budgets among drugs and other medical services in ways that produce the greatest health benefits to patients, regardless of component-specific budgets. In practice, this ideal is far from fully realized. Pharmacy directors still often focus on the pharmacy budget without due consideration of the impact on other budgets within the health plan. And to the extent that patients and employee benefit managers lack good outcomes information on which to evaluate different health plans, the incentives for providers to focus on comprehensive health outcomes rather than component budgets are not as strong as they should be. These systems, however, are relatively new, and management strategies and information systems are still evolving. Given the directions of structural change, there is good reason to be optimistic about the evolution in general of medical markets in the United States and, in particular, about the role of managed pharmacy benefits in these integrated delivery systems.

Competition between these integrated systems and looser, traditional indemnity plans should, in theory, preserve opportunities for consumers to express their willingness to pay for innovative drugs and, hence, preserve appropriate incentives for innovation. It is too early to judge how far this potential will be realized. But there is no doubt that the evolution of competitive health plans in the United States and their strategies for managing drug costs offer greater promise of achieving appropriate trade-offs between cost control and innovation than the regulatory systems of Europe. There, component budgeting is being superimposed on price and reimbursement controls. While global drug budgets may succeed in controlling drug spending where price regulation alone has failed, the combination violates the most basic incentive requirements for efficient use of medical resources today and efficient incentives for innovation for the future.

References

Association of the British Pharmaceutical Industry. 1993. *A Guide to the PPRS*. London: ABPI.

Averch, H., and L. L. Johnson. 1962. "Behavior of the Firm under Regulatory Constraint." *American Economic Review:* 1052–69.

Barral, P. E. 1990. *Fifteen Years of Pharmaceutical Research Results throughout the World (1975–1989)*. Paris: Fondation Rhone-Poulenc Sante.

———. 1995. *Twenty Years of Pharmaceutical Research Results throughout the World (1975–1994)*. Paris: Fondation Rhone-Poulenc Sante.

Berndt, E. R. 1994. *Uniform Pharmaceutical Pricing: An Economic Analysis*. Washington, D.C.: AEI Press.

Berndt, E. R., and D. M. Hesse. 1986. "Measuring and Assessing Capacity Utilization in the Manufacturing Sectors of Nine OECD Countries." *European Economic Review* 30: 961–89.

Brittan, Sir L. Speech on pharmaceutical pricing. European Commission press release, December 2, 1992.

Bureau Europeen des Unions de Consommateurs (BEUC). 1989. *Drug Prices and Drug Legislation in Europe*. Brussels.

Burstall, M. L., and B. G. Reuben. 1988. "The Cost of Non-Europe in the Pharmaceutical Industry." *Basic Findings* (15). Luxembourg: Commission of the European Communities.

Centre for Medicines Research. 1993. *Trends in Worldwide Pharmaceutical R&D Expenditure for the 1990s*. Carshalton, U.K.

Clarkson, K. V. 1996. "Intangible Capital and Profitability Measures: Effects of Research and Promotion on Rates of Return." In *Competitive Strategies in the Pharmaceutical Industry*, edited by R. B. Helms. Washington, D.C.: AEI Press.

Danzon, P. M. 1994. *The Effects of Regulation on the Pharmaceutical Industry*. Report to the Chaire D'Economie at Gestion de la Sante, Institut D'Etudes Politiques de Paris.

————. 1995. "The Economic Impact of Anti-Discount Pricing Legislation." Working paper. Health Care Systems Department, Wharton School, University of Pennsylvania, Philadelphia.

Danzon, P. M., L. G. Boothman, and P. E. Greenberg. 1995. "Consolidation and Restructuring: The Next Step in Managed Care." *Health Care Management Reviews* 2 (1): 1–15.

Danzon, P. M., and L. W. Chao. 1996. "Cross-national Price Differences for Pharmaceuticals: How Large and Why?" Working paper. Health Care Systems Department, Wharton School, University of Pennsylvania, Philadelphia.

Danzon, P. M., and J. D. Kim. 1996. "Price Indexes for Pharmaceuticals: How Accurate Are International Comparisons?" Working paper. Health Care Systems Department, Wharton School, University of Pennsylvania, Philadelphia.

Danzon, P. M., and H. Liu. 1996. "Reference Pricing and Physician Drug Budgets: The German Experience in Controlling Pharmaceutical Costs." Working paper. Health Care Systems Department, Wharton School, University of Pennsylvania, Philadelphia.

Danzon, P. M., and A. Percy. 1996. "The Effects of Price Regulation on Productivity in Pharmaceuticals." Working paper. Health Care Systems Department, Wharton School, University of Pennsylvania, Philadelphia.

Danzon, P. M., and D. Zhang. 1994. "Price Regulation in the Pharmaceutical Industry: Effects on Innovation." Working paper. Health Care Systems Department, Wharton School, University of Pennsylvania, Philadelphia.

DiMasi, J. A., H. G. Grabowski, and L. Lasagna. 1991. "The Cost of Innovation in the Pharmaceutical Industry." *Journal of Health Economics* 10: 107–42.

Dranove, D. 1988. "Pricing by Non-Profit Institutions: The Case of Hospital Cost Shifting." *Journal of Health Economics* 7: 47–57.

Ellis, R. P., and T. G. McGuire. 1993. "Supply-Side and Demand-Side Cost Sharing in Health Care." *Journal of Economic Perspectives* 131–51.

Gondek, K. 1994. "Prescription Drug Payment Policy: Past, Present and Future." *Health Care Financing Review.* Spring: 1–7.

Hancher, L. 1990. *Regulating the Competition: Government, Law and the Pharmaceutical Industry in the United Kingdom and France.* Oxford: Clarendon Press.

Ikegami, Naoki. Personal communication. 1995.

Maassen, B. M. 1995. *Reimbursement of Medicinal Products: The German Reference Price System Law, Administration and Practice and Economics.* Centre for New Europe: Zellik, Belgium.

Medical Ad News. Supplement. 1993. *100 Powerhouse Drugs.*

Morrisey, Michael A. 1994. *Cost Shifting in Health Care.* Washington, D.C.: AEI Press.

Myers, S., and N. S. Majluf. 1984. "Corporate Financing and Investment Decisions When Firms Have Information That Investors Do Not Have." *Journal of Financial Economics* 13: 187–221.

Pallot, P. 1992. "Fake Drug Fraud: Threat to Patients." *Daily Telegraph,* March 13.

Phelps, C. 1986. "Cross Subsidies and Charge Shifting in American Hospitals." In *Uncompensated Hospital Care,* edited by Frank A. Sloan, James F. Blumstein, and James M. Perrin, 108–25. Baltimore: Johns Hopkins University Press.

Ramsey, F. P. 1927. "A Contribution to the Theory of Taxation." *Economic Journal* 37: 47–61.

Redwood, H. 1993. *Price Regulation and Pharmaceutical Re-*

search: The Limits of Co-Existence. Felixstone, U.K.: Old-wicks Press Limited.

Rozek, R., and R. Rapp. 1992. "Parallel Trade in Pharmaceuticals: The Impact on Welfare and Innovation." Working Paper 16. National Economics Research Associates, Washington D.C.

Schulemberg, J. M., G.v.d., and O. Schaffski. 1993. "Implications of the Structural Reform of the Healthcare Act on the Referral and Hospital Admission Practices of Primary Care Physicians." Discussion Paper 34. University of Hanover Institute of Insurance Science.

Syndical National de L'Industrie Pharmaceutique (SNIP). 1993. *The Realities of the Pharmaceutical Industry in France.* Paris.

Thomas, L. G. III. 1994. "Implicit Industrial Policy: The Triumph of Britain and the Failure of France in Global Pharmaceuticals." *Industrial and Corporate Change* 3.

———. 1966. "Industrial Policy and International Competitiveness." In *Competitive Strategies in the Pharmaceutical Industry,* edited by R. B. Helms. Washington, D.C.: AEI Press.

U.S. Congressional Budget Office. 1994. *How Health Care Reform Affects Pharmaceutical R&D.* Washington, D.C.

U.S. General Accounting Office. 1992. *Prescription Drugs: Companies Typically Charge More in the U.S. Than in Canada.* GAO/HRD-92-110.

———. 1994a. *Prescription Drugs: Companies Typically Charge More in the U.S. Than in the United Kingdom.* GAO/HEHS 94-29.

———. 1994b. *Prescription Drug Spending Controls in Four European Countries.* GAO/HEHS 94-30.

U.S. Government Printing Office. 1993. *Health Security Act.* HR 3600 IH/S 1757 IS.

U.S. Office of Technology Assessment. 1993. *Pharmaceutical R&D: Costs, Risks and Rewards.* Washington, D.C. OTH-H-522.

Zeckhauser, R. 1970. "Medical Insurance: A Case Study of the Trade-off between Risk Spreading and Appropriate Incentives." *Journal of Economic Theory* 2: 10–26.

Index

About the Author

PATRICIA M. DANZON is the Celia Moh Professor of Health Care Systems and Insurance at the Wharton School of the University of Pennsylvania. She has held positions at the University of Chicago, Duke University, and the RAND Corporation.

The author is a fellow of the Institute of Medicine and the National Academy of Social Insurance. She has been a consultant on international health care issues to the World Bank, the New Zealand government, the Asian Development Bank, and the U.S. Agency for International Development.

Ms. Danzon received a B.A. from Oxford University and a Ph.D. in economics from the University of Chicago. She has been widely published in the fields of health care, insurance, and liability systems. The author is an adjunct scholar of the American Enterprise Institute.

William M. Landes
Clifton R. Musser Professor of
Economics
University of Chicago Law School

Sam Peltzman
Sears Roebuck Professor of Economics
and Financial Services
University of Chicago
Graduate School of Business

Nelson W. Polsby
Professor of Political Science
University of California at Berkeley

George L. Priest
John M. Olin Professor of Law and
Economics
Yale Law School

Murray L. Weidenbaum
Mallinckrodt Distinguished
University Professor
Washington University

Research Staff

Leon Aron
Resident Scholar

Claude E. Barfield
Resident Scholar; Director, Science
and Technology Policy Studies

Cynthia A. Beltz
Research Fellow

Walter Berns
Resident Scholar

Douglas J. Besharov
Resident Scholar

Robert H. Bork
John M. Olin Scholar in Legal Studies

Karlyn Bowman
Resident Fellow

Kenneth Brown
Visiting Fellow

John E. Calfee
Resident Scholar

Lynne V. Cheney
W. H. Brady, Jr., Distinguished Fellow

Stephen R. Conafay
Executive Fellow

Dinesh D'Souza
John M. Olin Research Fellow

Nicholas N. Eberstadt
Visiting Scholar

Mark Falcoff
Resident Scholar

John D. Fonte
Visiting Scholar

Gerald R. Ford
Distinguished Fellow

Murray F. Foss
Visiting Scholar

Diana Furchtgott-Roth
Assistant to the President and Resident
Fellow

Suzanne Garment
Resident Scholar

Jeffrey Gedmin
Research Fellow

Robert A. Goldwin
Resident Scholar

Robert W. Hahn
Resident Scholar

Robert B. Helms
Resident Scholar; Director, Health
Policy Studies

Glenn Hubbard
Visiting Scholar

Douglas Irwin
Henry Wendt Scholar in Political
Economy

James D. Johnston
Resident Fellow

Jeane J. Kirkpatrick
Senior Fellow; Director, Foreign and
Defense Policy Studies

Marvin H. Kosters
Resident Scholar; Director,
Economic Policy Studies

Irving Kristol
John M. Olin Distinguished Fellow

Dana Lane
Director of Publications

Michael A. Ledeen
Resident Scholar

James Lilley
Resident Fellow; Director, Asian
Studies Program

John H. Makin
Resident Scholar; Director, Fiscal
Policy Studies

Allan H. Meltzer
Visiting Scholar

Joshua Muravchik
Resident Scholar

Charles Murray
Bradley Fellow

Michael Novak
George F. Jewett Scholar in Religion,
Philosophy, and Public Policy;
Director, Social and
Political Studies

Norman J. Ornstein
Resident Scholar

Richard N. Perle
Resident Fellow

William Schneider
Resident Scholar

William Shew
Visiting Scholar

J. Gregory Sidak
F. K. Weyerhaeuser Fellow

Herbert Stein
Senior Fellow

Irwin M. Stelzer
Resident Scholar; Director, Regulatory
Policy Studies

Daniel Troy
Associate Scholar

W. Allen Wallis
Resident Scholar

Ben J. Wattenberg
Senior Fellow

Carolyn L. Weaver
Resident Scholar; Director, Social
Security and Pension Studies

A NOTE ON THE BOOK

This book was edited by Ann Petty
of the publications staff
of the American Enterprise Institute.
The index was prepared by Nancy H. Rosenberg,
and the figures were drawn by Hördur Karlsson.
The text was set in New Baskerville.
Coghill Composition Company, of
Richmond, Virginia, set the type,
and Data Reproductions Corporation, of
Rochester Hills, Michigan,
printed and bound the book,
using permanent acid-free paper.

The AEI Press is the publisher for the American Enterprise In-
stitute for Public Policy Research, 1150 Seventeenth Street,
N.W., Washington, D.C. 20036; *Christopher C. DeMuth,* publisher;
Dana Lane, director; *Ann Petty,* editor; *Leigh Tripoli,* editor; *Cheryl
Weissman,* editor; *Jennifer Lesiak,* editorial assistant.